A study of practical wisdom from two pas[t]
the trap of the Super-Pastor syndrome oft[e]
pastor and those who care about the healt[h]

TIMOTHY GEORGE
Research professor at Beeson Divinity Sch[ool]
General Editor of the 28-volume Reforma[tion]

"Be still my heart!" *Leveling the Church*—THIS is the church, body-life done God's way! *Leveling the Church* puts us on solid biblical ground and practically builds from there. I am so grateful our Father led Micah and Jeremy to write this much-needed practical manual where we learn God's plan for "equipping the saints for the work of ministry, to build up the body of Christ" (Eph. 4:12). May God use it to revive, engage, and mobilize His church in our sin-sick culture.

KAY ARTHUR
Cofounder, Brand Ambassador
Precept Ministries

The call to serve the church as a pastor is a call to equip the church unto service. That's precisely the message and the methods Micah Fries and Jeremy Maxfield point us to in this book, *Leveling the Church*. This book is spot-on and will benefit ministers and churches everywhere. I highly encourage you read it.

JASON ALLEN
President of Midwestern Baptist Theological Seminary

In this book, Micah Fries and Jeremy Maxfield dismantle the idea that the church is a corporation of consumers, served by a professional class. Instead, this book calls us back to an ancient vision of the New Testament: of a clergy called out not to serve in the place of the people but to equip and empower the people for the work of ministry. If we heed the call of this book, we will see a more faithful, more joyful, more purposeful church.

RUSSELL MOORE
President, The Ethics & Religious Liberty Commission of the Southern Baptist Convention

---

Too many pastors fall into the trap of trying to do everything themselves. Not only does it wear them out, it circumvents God's design for how the church should work. Micah Fries and Jeremy Maxfield challenge pastors to take seriously the biblical charge to "build up the body of Christ" so believers will be equipped and sent into ministry. That's when true multiplication begins to take place. Micah and Jeremy carefully identify the obstacles that prevent pastors and churches from multiplying themselves and offer practical solutions for clearing those hurdles. I'm grateful for this resource and hope others richly benefit from it.

KEVIN EZELL
President, North American Mission Board, SBC

We live in an era of notorious examples of bad leadership at every important institution of society, including the church. Many practitioners advocate a detached model of leadership that eschews the Bible's rich and consistent metaphor of shepherding. This is why *Leveling the Church* is such an important resource. Micah and Jeremy help pastors return to the biblical Ephesians 4 model of "equipping the saints for the work of ministry." If you want to mobilize your people for ministry, if you want to shepherd well, if you want to see a new generation of God's people empowered to live on mission, this book is for you. Buy this book and share it with your staff, your key lay volunteers, and anyone in a position of influence.

DANIEL DARLING
VP of Communications, ERLC, columnist, and author of several books, including *The Dignity Revolution*

I like this book a lot. I read it in a single reading! It lays out a faithful, biblical blueprint for how ministers ought to do ministry.

DANIEL L. AKIN
President of Southeastern Baptist Theological Seminary

What a delightful encouragement to read this refreshing new work from Micah Fries and Jeremy Maxfield! As indicated in the subtitle, this thoughtful book wisely guides readers toward a thoroughly biblical view of church and ministry, encouraging both a rethinking and reframing of what faithful leadership really means in our current context. The authors offer practical counsel and direction in each chapter, doing so in a theologically informed manner that is both timely and insightful. Highly recommended!

DAVID S. DOCKERY
Chancellor, Trinity Evangelical Divinity School

It is indeed a challenge. So many people see the pastor and staff of the church as the "hired hands" to do the work of ministry. Nothing could be further from the biblical truth. I am thankful to God for *Leveling the Church* by Micah Fries and Jeremy Maxfield. This book provides the needed road map for biblical equipping to take place. Read it. Apply it. Live it.

THOM S. RAINER
Founder and CEO of Church Answers
Author of *I Am a Church Member* and *Anatomy of a Revived Church*

Micah Fries and Jeremy Maxfield present an inspiring, compelling, and purely biblical vision of the church. As it has been in every generation, churches devoted to raising up ordinary people as gospel leaders hold the key to our future.

J. D. GREEAR
Pastor, The Summit Church, Raleigh-Durham, NC; 62nd president, The Southern Baptist Convention; author, *Gaining by Losing*

Leveling the Church is going to help you multiply what God wants to do in your church. Jesus will accomplish more through His body when you learn to do less and the congregation you serve is equipped for the work of ministry. Read this book and implement what you learn.

DERWIN L. GRAY
Lead Pastor, Transformation Church; author, *The High Definition Leader: Building Multiethnic Churches in a Multiethnic World*

All too often church members expect the pastor and paid staff to do the overwhelming amount of ministry in the local church. And overwhelming it is! Pastoral burnout is a common problem. Micah and Jeremy take us back to the biblical model of Christ's church, where every born-again believer has a clear role to fill through the use of their God-given gifts for the work of ministry. This is a book for pastors and members alike!

BRYANT WRIGHT
Senior Pastor, Johnson Ferry Baptist Church

LEVELING
THE CHURCH

Multiplying Your Ministry by Giving It Away

MICAH FRIES + JEREMY MAXFIELD

MOODY PUBLISHERS
CHICAGO

Unless otherwise indicated, Scripture quotations are from the CSB (Christian Standard Bible®), Copyright © 2017 by Holman Bible Publishers. Used by permission. Christian Standard Bible® and CSB® are federally registered trademarks of Holman Bible Publishers.

Scripture quotations marked HCSB are taken from the Holman Christian Standard Bible®, Used by Permission HCSB ©1999, 2000, 2002, 2003, 2009 Holman Bible Publishers. Holman Christian Standard Bible®, Holman CSB®, and HCSB® are federally registered trademarks of Holman Bible Publishers.

Scripture quotations marked ESV are from The Holy Bible, English Standard Version® (ESV®), copyright © 2001 by Crossway, a publishing ministry of Good News Publishers. Used by permission. All rights reserved.

Scripture quotations marked NIV are taken from the Holy Bible, New International Version®, NIV®. Copyright © 1973, 1978, 1984, 2011 by Biblica, Inc.™ Used by permission of Zondervan. All rights reserved worldwide. www.zondervan.com. The "NIV" and "New International Version" are trademarks registered in the United States Patent and Trademark Office by Biblica, Inc.™

Scripture quotations marked KJV are taken from the King James Version.

Edited by Kevin P. Emmert
Interior Design: Ragont Design
Cover Design: Faceout Studios
Cover illustration of church icon copyright © 2018 by M-vector / Shutterstock (455165260).
Cover illustration of line pattern copyright © 2019 by TechSolution / Shutterstock (538648516).
All rights reserved for all of the above photos.
Author photo for Jeremy Maxfield: Shaq Hardy

Library of Congress Cataloging-in-Publication Data

Names: Fries, Micah, author.
Title: Leveling the church : multiplying your ministry by giving it away /
   Micah Fries and Jeremy Maxfield.
Description: Chicago : Moody Publishers, 2020. | Includes bibliographical
   references. | Summary: "What if the secret to pastoral success is to do
   less ministry? Micah Fries and Jeremy Maxfield argue that a pastor's
   true goal should be to equip the so-called ordinary members of their
   church to take on these pastoral tasks. And in Leveling the Church,
   they'll show you how."--
   Provided by publisher.
Identifiers: LCCN 2019028695 (print) | LCCN 2019028696 (ebook) | ISBN
   9780802418777 (paperback) | ISBN 9780802497512 (ebook)
Subjects: LCSH: Pastoral theology. | Discipling (Christianity)
Classification: LCC BV4011.3 .F75 2020 (print) | LCC BV4011.3 (ebook) |
   DDC 253--dc23
LC record available at https://lccn.loc.gov/2019028695
LC ebook record available at https://lccn.loc.gov/2019028696

All websites and phone numbers listed herein are accurate at the time of publication but may change in the future or cease to exist. The listing of website references and resources does not imply publisher endorsement of the site's entire contents. Groups and organizations are listed for informational purposes, and listing does not imply publisher endorsement of their activities.

ISBN: 978-0-8024-1877-7

Originally delivered by fleets of horse-drawn wagons, the affordable paperbacks from D. L. Moody's publishing house resourced the church and served everyday people. Now, after more than 125 years of publishing and ministry, Moody Publishers' mission remains the same—even if our delivery systems have changed a bit. For more information on other books (and resources) created from a biblical perspective, go to: www.moodypublishers.com or write to:

Moody Publishers
820 N. LaSalle Boulevard
Chicago, IL 60610

1 3 5 7 9 10 8 6 4 2

Printed in the United States of America

To pastors who have cared for me and who helped
me understand the ideas contained in this book:
Gary Wiggins, Vernon Armitage, and John Marshall.
You men have epitomized faithful service.
MICAH

To the "D-Team" staff, volunteers, and interns at Brainerd.
You are more than leaders, you are family.
JEREMY

CONTENTS

Chapter 1

RETHINKING LEADERSHIP

I failed. Those who knew me at the time didn't realize it, but I failed.*

It was my first position as a Senior Pastor. Many of my wife's family members had been raised in that small, rural congregation. Some of them continued to fill the pews of the little white church building each week. They had called me as their pastor when I was an eager but inexperienced twenty-four-year-old. I didn't know what I was doing. My preparation included a theology degree from a Bible college and growing up as a pastor's son. I had served as a youth pastor for a few years before moving overseas as a church planter in West Africa. That missionary adventure was cut short after a rough bout with malaria, kidney stones, and a few other afflictions stripped me down to a pasty white, six-foot-six inch skeleton. My wife and I were encouraged to return home, wondering what God had in store for us. What would we do?

When I took over the little church, I was desperate for it to succeed. I wanted to see people believe in Jesus and discipled into His image. I wanted us to commit to a lifestyle of missions

---

* Unless noted otherwise, "I" always refers to Micah, though Jeremy is equally a coauthor of this book.

and invest our lives in others. Judging from the numbers, we succeeded. We more than doubled our weekly attendance. The church was more than a hundred years old and had never had any staff members outside of a bivocational pastor, and we added two bivocational staff members during my time there. The budget grew substantially. These are all wonderful things, but because of the pressure that I placed on myself, I made some critical errors. I exhausted myself in trying to do everything. To so many people watching, the church and my leadership might have looked successful, and yet ultimately, I failed.

Did you notice how many times the word *I* appeared in that last paragraph? Even my best intentions for gospel ministry were wrapped up in my own misunderstanding of success. Even what I did for Jesus was about *me*. I didn't just want the church to succeed. *I* wanted to succeed. That is why I failed.

A Biblical Plan

The biblical plan for church leadership is to develop a culture of multiplication: to not only see people come to faith, but also help them grow into maturity. A large part of that maturity is learning how to minister to others. This ministry leads to them becoming more like Christ. This shouldn't be surprising, and yet too often it is. The Bible is pretty clear on this point, and yet you would be hard-pressed to find a pastoral job description that lists personal discipleship and multiplication of ministry leaders as a primary responsibility. God never intended Lone Ranger pastors to save the day, charging into ministry on their own. It's a childhood fantasy to believe that we can pull ourselves up by our spiritual bootstraps, flash a perfect smile, and be everyone's hero. While a leader may get away with riding solo for a while, even earning a legendary mystique as more-than-human, ministry was never intended to be done alone. You can't—and shouldn't—do it all.

Unfortunately, many of us have developed a pattern, particularly in the American church, that perpetuates this myth of heroic individualism in ministry. We've even nuanced our verbiage to reflect it. When a pastor does ministry, we tend to describe their behavior as "pastoral." We might say things like, "Pastor so-and-so is especially pastoral." What we mean is that they are good at serving the ministry needs of others. This is unfortunate. Scripture seems to indicate that church leaders are not called primarily to do ministry themselves as much as they are called to prepare and deploy the church to do ministry.

Does this mean that pastors are not called to personally serve the people in their churches and communities? Of course not. However, this is not their unique calling as pastors. They ought to lead the way in ministry but not as their primary vocational responsibility. Ministry is our familial responsibility as church members. Multiplication is our vocational responsibility as church leaders. All Christians are expected to serve one another, and as

> **Ministry is our familial responsibility as church members. Multiplication is our vocational responsibility as church leaders.**

pastors we should lead the way. But it is not solely our job to do ministry.

In the upcoming pages, I, along with my coauthor Jeremy Maxfield, will make the case that "doing" ministry is part of our familial responsibility shared with every believer in the church. It is to be expected, then, that we select our leaders from among those who "do" ministry well. But it is also clear in Scripture that our leaders are not called to spend all their time doing, in isolation, and instead are called to develop the church so that we all do ministry together. Consider Ephesians 4:11–16:

> And He personally gave some to be apostles, some prophets, some evangelists, some pastors and teachers, for the training of the saints in the work of ministry, to build up the body of Christ, until we all reach unity in the faith and in the knowledge of God's Son, growing into a mature man with a stature measured by Christ's fullness. Then we will no longer be little children, tossed by the waves and blown around by every wind of teaching, by human cunning with cleverness in the techniques of deceit. But speaking the truth in love, let us grow in every way into Him who is the head—Christ. From Him the whole body, fitted and knit together by every supporting ligament, promotes the growth of the body for building up itself in love by the proper working of each individual part. (HCSB)

Here, the apostle Paul shares the secret to success—true success. It's literally spelled out for us—*Church Leadership for Dummies*, as it were. We are called "for the training of the saints in the work of ministry." The first-century missionary and church planter lets us all in on the scorecard. It hasn't changed in the nearly two thousand years since Paul was inspired by the Holy Spirit to write these words. There are no hacks, shortcuts, or formulas, but we do have a clear picture of what it means to win. We have a clear goal as leaders despite the transient fads and current buzzwords.

The text lays out four simple truths about church leaders and their responsibility to the church that are revolutionary when we take them seriously. So, before we review the four points introduced in Ephesians, ask yourself, *Am I ready to take these seriously?*

Honestly, are we more interested in our own measures of success or in a biblical perspective? Will we have the courage to allow God's Word to flip our understanding upside down in order to set it right side up? Are we ready to consider whether our best intentions and efforts may look impressive but ultimately lead to us failing in our true calling as leaders?

You may have noticed that Paul identified several leadership roles, pastor being just one of them. Throughout this book the terms *pastor* and *leader* will often be used interchangeably for our purposes within the local church context. The reason for this is that the roles of apostles, prophets, and evangelists are given primarily for the work of spreading and unifying new churches, while the roles of pastors and teachers are given for the growth and unity of members of the churches themselves.

This brings us to our first point: these roles of leadership are *given*.

And He personally gave

First, God gives leaders to the church. Leaders are not in their role simply because of giftedness or desire, though both of those things are important (see 1 Tim. 3). Leaders exist in their roles, first and foremost, because God has ordained that they be there. A church leader's role is a commission, an assignment from the God of the universe.[1]

This means that we must take our ministry leadership roles seriously—as a matter of responsibility and obedience. It's vital that we pay particular attention to what the scriptural text directs us to do in our leadership roles. We must not get distracted from our assignments, nor can we approach them with halfhearted efforts. Let's ensure that we're accomplishing the specific work that God has assigned us.

The text says more than that leaders are simply given to the church though. It specifically says that leaders are given as a personal gift from God. The seemingly redundant wording of the sentence emphasizes the personal nature of what God has given. God not only gave, but He *personally* gave. This is a gift characteristic of God Himself, as an overflow of who He is. The idea here is that church leaders are intended by God to be a good and gracious gift to the church. Now, we wouldn't recommend that you stand before your congregation on Sunday and tell them that, as a leader, you are God's gift to them. That probably wouldn't go well! But you ought to find tremendous encouragement, confidence, and hope in the fact that you have been given a specific task by God, and that your work is a blessing.

While church leadership is a blessing, it is not easy. Serving the church is difficult. It is often lonely. It typically does not pay very well, and it can prove challenging for your family. In the midst of all of this, you will find yourself needing this encouraging truth from Ephesians 4:11. When challenging times come, you should reflect on this passage. God, in His authority and goodness, has ordained that your position would exist and that you would lead His church. What's more, in God's good providence, He intended for you to be His good gift to the church, and He intended the church to be a good gift to you, to your marriage, to your family, and more.

As leaders, it is essential that we guard the integrity of leadership as the precious gift that it is. We must surround ourselves with accountability in community. We must measure our lives in faithfulness to the Word of God. Unfortunately, it is possible, and far too prevalent, that this doesn't prove to be true in practice. Pastoral malpractice exists, and it can be devastating. Whether it be moral failure, leadership failure, theological failure, or some other type of failure, a specific pastor or leader can prove to be detrimental to the congregation they lead. When this happens, however, it should be clear that this contradicts God's intended good design for the church and her leaders. God's design is one of mutual blessing.

We must acknowledge that congregational malpractice also exists and has destroyed too many good leaders. This is why when hiring new staff or training new leaders, even in a healthy congregation, the inevitability of eventual disappointment, conflict, and pain should always be clearly stated up front. Because of the intimate, personal nature of faith, the sting of pain from a church relationship can be among the greatest any person can experience. Yet again, however, when it happens, it happens in direct contradiction to the design that God intends for His church and her leaders.

The church is one, big, sometimes-dysfunctional family. But we are a family nonetheless. The church is given by God to be a blessing for us all—a good gift of His grace in our lives. He Himself has given you to His church for His purpose. The church is not yours; she's His. But He has entrusted her to your care. Be a blessing. Love the church like you love God Himself. He personally gave you to one another.

. . . for the training of the saints in the work of ministry

Second, knowing that leaders are given at the pleasure of God, it is important to ask what the task of the leader is. What does it mean, practically speaking, to love and bless the church to whom you've been given? While any honest response would affirm that this requires a multifaceted answer, the answer for the purpose of this book and the one explicit in this specific text is that leaders equip the body. God gives leaders to the church, but He doesn't give the church leaders so that they can do all of the ministry. This distinction is vital to both leaders and churches.

As mentioned earlier, we have unwittingly modified our vocabulary to indicate that when we serve the needs of others, we are typically known as being "pastoral." This gives away a subtle but dangerous belief that what it means to be distinctly pastoral is to minister to the needs of others. It allows us to make nonsensical statements like: "pastor so-and-so is not very pastoral." Technically, being pastoral in that sense would be one of many characteristics or qualifications for a pastor, one that could be pretty far down the priority list or even omitted as "preferred but not required" on the job description.

The biblical definition of what it means to be a pastor has been hijacked and corrupted. Sadly, we've done it to ourselves. It's tempting for pastors to serve as little more than entertainers or CEOs, regardless of a church's size or style. We have defined pastoral leadership in a consumer-driven context in which the pastor is viewed as a professional dispenser of religious goods and services, and congregants are viewed as spiritual consumers who simply sit back and have their needs cared for. The job of the churches—and therefore the jobs of the pastors as paid professionals—is to meet the needs of anyone who comes through the door.

While this may make the pastor seem noble, and while the pastor should certainly be a servant, we actually do a tragic disservice to other individuals, the church as a whole, and the kingdom of God if we personally do the ministry that God has called the whole church to do. Not only that, the Bible is clear that the ministry won't be done well and that the church will not flourish when we assume this philosophy of the professional service provider.

Please don't make my mistake. God does not expect you to "do ministry" as your vocational responsibility. This certainly is a controversial statement in our contemporary church environment. In a few chapters, we'll dig into this more deeply. But for now, let's be clear: pastors and church leaders don't minister to the needs of the church as their *vocational* responsibility, but they do minister to the needs of the church as part of their *familial* responsibility. God has given the church—and every member of it—to minister to the needs of the body. Ministry is our collective responsibility. It is for this reason that I don't use the title "Minister" for myself or anyone else on our church staff who is paid to work for the church. We do not allocate "ministry" to the compensated few. Instead, we recognize that leaders of the church—including the paid pastoral staff—are tasked with equipping the entire church to serve the needs of the body together.

Paul said that the role of the pastor is to train the saints for the work of ministry. It couldn't be clearer. Church members are all called to do the work of ministry. The distinct calling and role of pastors is training, equipping, and multiplying the workers. As the lead teacher, your role is not to simply teach people in the church what they need to know but to train people for what they can do as the church.

Did you notice the other title or name given in the text? It's easy to skim over what is arguably the most important identity mentioned in this paragraph. We are prone to prioritize roles of leadership as exceptional, but the most incredible and intrinsically valuable description of personal identity and position is the one we all share—saints. We have all been set apart as holy for God's purpose, united as one body. This is a major theme throughout Paul's letter to the Ephesian church. The great mystery of God has been revealed. He is creating a new people for Himself. Saints. The body of Christ. When that transformative reality sinks in, when we "comprehend with all the saints what is the length and width, height and depth of God's love" (Eph. 3:18 HCSB), it completely demol-ishes our tendency to prop up a leader on a pedestal. Instead, we rally together to build up the col-lective body of Christ. The goal is no longer a select few profes-sional Christians but an entirely united congregation of mature Christians.

God is fully pleased with you through the completed work of Jesus, not an overloaded work schedule. Doing everything yourself does not honor Christ or help the church.

Leader, remember that your identity in Christ is not pastor—it is saint, just like the people you serve. God is fully pleased with you through the completed work of Jesus, not an overloaded work schedule. Doing everything yourself does not honor Christ or help the church. Share the load. Empower others. Lead by humble example as one part among many. Your posi-tion is not primarily defined in relation to being over other church members; it is primarily defined in relation to being under Christ. Together, each part of the body works in unison with the head. God Himself has given you to the church, not to do all the work yourself but to train the saints for the work of ministry.

. . . we will no longer be little children
When God gives leaders to the church and the leaders invest their time in developing the body to do ministry together, the

body is built up. We grow—not just in size, but in stature. Maturity is the goal. The purpose of leaders is to help everyone grow up. It's what Paul identified as a driving passion in his letter to another church, in Colossae: "We proclaim Him, warning and teaching everyone with all wisdom, so that we may present everyone mature in Christ" (Col. 1:28 HCSB).

In God's economy, the ability of the church to mature into the image of Jesus shares a dependent relationship with leadership who is training and handing off ministry. This seems counterintuitive compared to our often typical practices in the church. We have developed a pattern of expecting maturity before we give people ministry responsibilities. Functionally, it's as if we are expecting people to grow in strength by reading nutrition labels and identifying exercise routines without ever developing healthy eating habits and practicing the movements they see. Maturity is the end game. We train to win. And we can't win until everyone gets in the game to play their part.

In Ephesians 4, Paul wants us to understand that unless we turn people loose with ministry responsibilities, they will never grow into maturity. In other words, growth in theology and practice occurs as people get their hands dirty, scrape their knees, and share their lives in ministry. Your job is to be the coach, not the star player. At most, you're the quarterback leading a team down the field. You're the captain of the team, first among equals. You direct other players, read the situation, and keep everyone focused together in order to reach your common goal. No matter how talented you are, you'll never succeed if you keep the ball and try to run it every time you line up. Sometimes you may see an opportunity to charge toward your goal, but most of the time you're handing things off or passing them to other players who are open. Your team doesn't exist to help you win. Your job is to help the team win.

There are too many armchair quarterbacks. The Christian life is not one of passive spectators or even opinionated fans. We all are players. Pastor and author Jim Putman of Real Life Ministries has popularized the saying that church is a team sport.[2] The apostle Paul said something similar centuries before when writing that leaders are tasked with "equipping the saints for the work of ministry, to build up the body of Christ, until we all reach unity in the faith and in the knowledge of God's Son, growing into maturity with a stature measured by Christ's fullness. Then we will no longer be little children." The goal is growth. Success is measured by maturity.

We live in a church era built on the foundations laid in the age of enlightenment. For generations, there has been an unspoken core belief that education in a classroom setting is the primary pathway to growth and success. Sunday school traces its origin back to this time period of the late 1800s. While this form of group education absolutely has value, it's time for us to move away from such a narrow model of functional relationships as dispensers and consumers of religious information. This does not diminish the importance of structured educational growth; it actually magnifies it by rightly repositioning it as a formative part of holistic growth and maturity. It's part of what Colin Marshall and Tony Payne have so helpfully described as the trellis and the vine.[3] A gardener's objective is fruitful growth, not the construction of rigid structures in the garden. Any good gardener—and any good pastor—knows that flourishing requires intentionality. Otherwise all of our labor is fruitless or, at best, unsustainable. We're just working up a sweat and staying busy without any real plan or application of wisdom over time.

Be good teachers. Prepare and deliver well-crafted sermons. The pulpit ministry of the church should obviously maintain a place of prominence in our churches. This is essential in congregational life. However, we have to abandon the mindset that just delivering the Word clearly and offering classes that teach the right lessons are sufficient to lead people to Christlikeness. The Word itself would contradict that (see 1 Cor. 12:13; 2 Cor. 1:21–22; Col. 3:16; James 1:25; 1 Peter 2:9–12; Heb. 10:24). In our church, we summarize our ministry strategy this way: we deliver the Word, disciple the believer, and deploy the church. There's an ongoing and intentional effort to not only educate, but also to emulate and replicate. It's not enough to teach if we aren't growing into maturity and reproducing through multiplication.

We have to grasp the specific ways that the church grows when the leadership equips the body to do ministry, rather than simply doing the ministry for the body. They grow in unity, knowledge, doctrinal stability, gracious speech, and the character of Jesus. Each of these is directly tied to ministry experience, helping us understand why God underscores the priority of church leaders developing church members for ministry.

Let us grow in every way into Him who is the head—Christ

Finally, when God gives leaders to the church and the leaders invest their time developing other church members to serve in ministry, everyone grows up and, ultimately, Jesus gets the glory. We live in the days of the Super Pastor (we'll address Super Pastor more in chapter 6). The Super Pastor platforms well. He has a large following. He appears to have it all together and appears able to do just about anything. However, what the Super Pastor doesn't realize is that he is crippling the church he leads. When all eyes are on him and he performs on behalf of both Jesus and the church, everyone's growth is stunted, the church body atrophies from inactivity, and he is blindly headed for a disappointing fall. Though most Super Pastors may not realize the damage they are doing, I believe that they do realize that their life is a mirage. It's a fairy tale without the happy ending. There's no way that storyline finishes well. But leaders may genuinely be deceived into thinking that it's their job— their calling from God even—to keep up their appearances in order to lead others. A desire for increasing numbers will tolerate an increasing numbness. Soon, everyone is settling for a good show rather than active participation in the life-giving body of Christ.

As pastors, we aren't nearly as gifted as we often portray ourselves to be. And for some leaders, this facade eventually comes crashing down, hurting the pastor, their family, and occasionally tearing the church apart that they were trying so desperately to hold together. The saddest thing about all this is not that the church leader has built a fragile house of cards. No, the saddest part is that the pastor, too often, gets the glory. Super Pastors develop super followings of people who adore them—even idolize them. And as unhealthy as that is for the pastor, for those who follow the pastor, and for the churches they serve, the greatest harm done is the damage done to the name and reputation of God.

However, in a church where a pastor is doing what he is supposed to—developing the members for ministry—the body collectively serves together, not allowing for any one person to get the credit, thus pointing to God as the Creator and Sustainer of all things. All this ministry is done as Jesus enables it to be so, and it is done to bring Him great glory. Notice the pattern in Ephesians 4:11–16:

- Jesus brings the church together (unity in diversity)
- Jesus makes the church grow
- Jesus increases the church's capacity to love
- Jesus helps every believer reach his or her potential

This is the dream for every church leader I know. This is what we really want when we allow ourselves and our mistaken measures of success to get out of the way. We want the church to grow into, and to be, every one of these things. Could it be that God gave us a plan to make it happen, but we've naively sought to move on and improve on it through more recent history? Have we been seduced by business models, marketing principles, and growth strategies and forgotten our true love and the seemingly paradoxical truth of God's Word?

Our Purpose

The aim of this book is not to point fingers at anyone. The desire is simply to point to Scripture and ask whether our leadership and churches resemble what we see in the text. We will display a biblical model that leads to discipleship and leadership development, and unleashes the church to serve on mission. We don't have all the answers for you, just like we don't have all the answers for the church we serve. But we believe we're asking the right question and looking in the right direction, even as we clumsily seek to move toward active and intentional growth in maturity through multiplication. We grow by letting go.

I started this chapter—and this book—by confessing that I had failed. I didn't develop members for ministry. Sure, there were occasional examples. Some of the wonderful people I pastored would probably stick up for me and disagree with my analysis. But I know what I did. And more specifically, I know now what I *didn't* do. I know that in my stress-fueled push to see the church grow and "get everything right," I often took ministry responsibilities away from people so that I could do them myself. I determined that I could do things better, more quickly, or more easily by myself than if I taught someone else do it. Consequently, I not only preached weekly and developed vision and strategies for the church but also found myself designing and printing the bulletins, weekly. I would regularly get to church early on a Sunday morning to sweep out the foyer. I ultimately tried to have my hands on every area of the church ministry. And, if I'm, honest, I still struggle with this. Grabbing a broom or lending a helping hand isn't a problem; not being willing and able to let go is.

The upshot of my efforts was that the church did grow. People around me would pat me on the back. Others would tell me they admired my ministry. But I know that I failed. I did the ministry instead of developing and deploying the church to do ministry. Instead of developing and discipling a committed core of church leaders, in some senses I left the church in worse leadership shape when I left than when I came, even though there was more money and more people. As painful as it is for me to admit it, it's also cathartic. I failed. But thank God that He shows grace, and I don't have to continue failing to be intentional in that way as I've moved forward as a pastor.

Even while writing this book, I don't pretend to be the shining example of leadership success. My struggles aren't all past tense. The church I serve is not without its challenges. I still experience the growing pains of pastoral responsibilities and don't know whether I'm making all the right decisions. But I can say with confidence that Jeremy and I believe wholeheartedly in the purpose of leadership laid out in this book. He and I have seen the fruit of multiplying leaders as we both served other churches while working for LifeWay in Nashville, and even more recently as we served together on the lead pastoral team for Brainerd Baptist Church in Chattanooga. We'll share more about what we have learned, how we've seen God work, and where we've made mistakes. But most of all, we pray that you'll be encouraged and emboldened to stop trying to do everything yourself. You can't do it all. You shouldn't do it all. The more you try to hang on to ministry, the more you hold back the ministry. Unleash your church!

Our prayer is that you can learn from the Word of God and from what we've learned to be the true measure of success as a pastor. Are you doing great work, but doing it all yourself? Or are you equipping and empowering others? Are you continually adding one more thing to your agenda? Or are you multiplying ministry? Are people growing in maturity? Are they looking to Jesus and looking more like Jesus?

You have a unique responsibility. Do what God has called you to do—what He personally gave you to the church to do. Create a culture of multiplication by narrowing your focus. Look at who you are developing. Start doing less ministry by yourself whenever you can include someone else. Don't spend all of your time visiting hospitals, counseling people, and preparing for funerals without taking others along with you. By adding someone to your usual activities, you no longer carry 100 percent of the weight for the ministry tasks previously done alone. Eventually, others are not only helping 50/50 in what you do, but twice as much ministry will begin to happen without your invitation or supervision. When you focus on development so that you're not the only person "doing" ministry on behalf of the church, you've multiplied your impact—and your longevity in ministry—exponentially. They see, then share, then spread ministry beyond your limited capacity to be everywhere and to do everything. Do less ministry. Develop more people. Deploy your people for the good of the church and the glory of Jesus' name.

Chapter 2

REFRAMING LEADERSHIP SUCCESS

How in the world do we measure success in the church? Is it faithfulness? Is it numerical growth? Is it more baptisms? Is it more disciples? Is it larger offerings?

In his book *Center Church*, Timothy Keller contends that most people view church leadership through the lens of "success" (more people, higher offerings, and so on), or through the lens of "faithfulness" (preaching the Word, staying consistent, and more). Keller, as he is wont to do, offers an alternative. He contends that *fruitfulness* should be the goal:

> As I read, reflected, and taught, I came to the conclusion that a more biblical theme for ministerial evaluation than either success or faithfulness is *fruitfulness*. Jesus, of course, told his disciples that they were to "bear much fruit" (John 15:8). Paul spoke even more specifically. He spoke of conversions as "fruit" when he desired to preach in Rome "that I might have some fruit among you also, even as among other Gentiles" (Rom 1:13 KJV). Paul also spoke of the "fruit" of godly character that a minister can see growing in Christians under his care. This included the "fruit of the Spirit"

(Gal 5:22). Good deeds, such as mercy to the poor, are called "fruit" as well (Rom 15:28).[1]

I tend to agree with Keller. While many of the measurements that we currently employ are not bad or wrong, they are incomplete. We measure "success" with metrics like attendance and baptisms, and we should. These are helpful indicators. We also measure "faithfulness" with metrics like tenure and fidelity to Scripture, and we should. These are also helpful indicators. But there is more. And as we saw in chapter 1, God is calling church leaders to something more than we see in the typical evangelical church. He is calling us to not only preach, but also help develop those who are in our church—not just in their knowledge of the Word, but in their application of the Word. We are being called to help produce disciples who know the Word and obey it.

I grow concerned when I hear people say things like, "Just preach the Word, and the church will be fine." To be clear, I'm not denigrating biblical preaching. I'm an expository, verse-by-verse preacher who would preach for forty-five-plus minutes every week if time constraints weren't a factor. I love and believe in biblical preaching. But it is inconsistent with the Bible's model and teaching for pastoral leadership to assume that preaching alone, no matter how rich and biblical it may be, is sufficient for church health. Too often, our truncated view of church leadership and health means that we create churches that are little more than a seminary and a show. Yes, there's great preaching and the music is out of this world, but where are the disciples? By all means, insist on faithful, biblical preaching. Just don't think that preaching alone is a silver bullet. Jesus' model of sending the disciples out, as seen in passages like Luke 9 and 10, displays for us that Jesus not only taught but also believed in the importance of obedience and ministry engagement in the discipleship process.

This shouldn't surprise us. This is precisely what James calls us to. The half brother of Jesus, once a skeptic who became a devoted follower of Jesus and

Too often, our truncated view of church leadership and health means that we create churches that are little more than a seminary and a show. Yes, there's great preaching and the music is out of this world, but where are the disciples?

leader of the church, knew that knowledge about God and the Bible was wasted unless it was accompanied by a changed and devoted life of ministry service: "For just as the body without the spirit is dead, so also faith without works is dead" (James 2:26 HCSB). This is no small statement. Faith without works is dead. If there is no accompanying life change, there is no faith in the first place.

Consider now how we measure our effectiveness in the church. If we measure effectiveness based on these biblical metrics—namely, that God is calling church leaders to develop the members to do ministry, and if they are not living out their faith in action, they have no faith at all—then the real win is not just seeing more people in our churches (though that is good) but multiplying them in ministry effectiveness, thus establishing both our leadership effectiveness and the genuineness of their own faith.

If our understanding of "the win" is going to reflect this revised understanding of effectiveness, then how should we rethink pastoral development? Should we expect a different process as we call, train, and send out pastors and church leaders? I believe that pastoral development—leadership development—should not only reflect increasing knowledge in the study of Scripture, theology, the original languages, and church history, but it should also reflect the "so what?" Our teaching should lead to changed lives, our leadership development should lead to better leaders. In other words, once we have learned some important elements of Scripture, theology, languages, or church history, we must follow that up by asking, "So what?" To what end do we study these things?

Consider the example of Jesus in Luke 9. After having walked with them and taught them for an extended period of time, Jesus sent them out. He sent them out with authority and responsibility, and He expected them to embody the teaching that He had invested in them. "Summoning the Twelve, He gave them power and authority over all the demons, and power to heal diseases. Then he sent them to proclaim the kingdom of God and to heal the sick" (Luke 9:1–2 HCSB). He was calling them to not only learn from Him but also to do as He did. They were His representatives on the earth. Jesus did this, of course, because He knew that the day was coming when He would not be there. They needed to be prepared to function in His absence. Further, though, Jesus did this because they were His plan to reach the world. He was investing in disciples so the world could be transformed by His gospel. And in the book of Acts, we see evidence of this occurring. In Acts 17:6–7, we see the story of Paul and other disciples continuing to do what Jesus had sent out the original disciples to do in Luke 9: they were proclaiming the kingdom of God. Acts 17:6–7 reads, "When they did not find them, they dragged Jason and some of the brothers before the city officials, shouting, 'These men who have turned the world upside down have come here too, and Jason has received them as guests! They are all acting contrary to Caesar's decrees, saying that there is another king—Jesus'" (HCSB). These disciples, who were disciples of the original disciples (generational multiplication), had taken Jesus' words seriously, and the world was being changed because of it.

If Scripture points us so clearly in this direction, then why would we resist resetting our own scorecard? Often, our reluctance traces back to expectations and applause. First, there is our history. Over the years, our vision of pastoral leadership, and church leadership, has strayed from this New Testament expectation to a belief that the pastor is the paid professional whose job is to serve the needs of the church. Beyond that, we have expectations. Connected closely to our history are the expectations of our churches. Our churches often function like consumers who think they have a right to expect what they want from the pastor. Biblical expectations can be pushed to the side when they conflict with the congregation's desire to have a pastor or church leader whose job is to serve their needs. This, then, becomes difficult for the pastor or congregation to resist, as their job is often tied to meeting membership expectations. Finally, there is the issue of applause. For pastors and church leaders, using

> **What we measure determines how we behave. If we don't reset the scorecard, we won't have a church that reflects God's purposes for His church.**

more traditional metrics like attendance as the primary barometer of success can lead to foregoing other concerns in an attempt to win the applause of other pastors, church members, or denominational or network leadership.

All this underscores one of the most important functional realities in the church: our metrics determine our behavior, every single time. Remember this, what we measure determines how we behave. If we don't reset the scorecard, we won't have a church that reflects God's purposes for His church.

Resetting the Scorecard

Here's what I mean by resetting the scorecard to measure holistic development and not just bottom-line growth. Jeremy and I served together for several years of transition at Brainerd Baptist Church in Chattanooga, Tennessee. While no church is perfect and each has its struggles, most of what we could consider the major building blocks were part of the DNA when we joined the leadership team. The church already valued biblical preaching and teaching, personal discipleship, and fulfilling the Great Commission. This threefold priority was summed up as follows:

Deliver the Word
Disciple the Believer
Deploy the Church

Interestingly, members of our Personnel Team pointed out that in God's providence, the three most recent pastors of the church each had a heart for these Three Ds, but with a unique passion for one area of emphasis. My passion is to multiply and mobilize people for the sake of mission (Deploy). Before me, Robby Gallaty had a passion for making disciples who will make disciples (Disciple). Before him, Darryl Craft had a passion for evangelism and expository preaching (Deliver). It's amazing to see how God was leading our entire congregation in holistic development, not just numerical growth.

Over the past two decades, as the city has grown and the church's focus has narrowed, we've experienced tremendous growth in attendance, giving, and facilities. Each of these bottom-line numbers show an upward trend, and we celebrate each of these markers of growth. But getting bigger is not always the same as growing healthier. As parents we love to see our children grow, but if we measure only height and weight, we reach a point where bigger numbers can be misleading and even detrimental to the goal of raising vibrant children who can flourish on their own.

About a decade ago, the church shifted major attention to getting church members into D-Groups or discipleship groups. The law of exponential growth proved true as unthinkable numbers of men and women participated in these intentional environments for personal discipleship. At one point, the total number of people who had been in D-Groups was approximately 80 percent of weekend worship attendance. Our purpose in this book isn't to go into the dynamics of a particular model of organizing ministry, but I bring this up to show that this was one of the first major and measurable shifts in our church family beyond the usual numbers of worship attendance, budget, buildings, and even Sunday school. When something new was measured and celebrated, the church responded.[2]

Coming in to lead the church after a year between pastors, Jeremy and I noticed that as the one area had been emphasized, people became less clear on their need for ongoing biblical community in what we call Life Groups. More people were taking ownership of their spiritual lives. On the other hand, without steady community and after a year of an interim pastor and no discipleship pastor, there seemed to be as many definitions for discipleship and different expectations for members as there were individuals in the church. This middle piece of community between the pulpit and personal discipleship was like a muscle that hadn't been exercised—at least not as intentionally as the other two areas of preaching and discipleship, especially during the interim. If we were going to grow again in our new season as a church, we would need to add some new measures now that the pieces had been instilled into the DNA of the church body. The rule was clearly working, for better and for worse: what you measure will determine behavior.

We began a fresh emphasis on "what" we would be about—developing and multiplying new leaders. It soon became clear that as familiar as the Three Ds were among our church staff and congregation, we needed to re-clarify our "why" and remind everyone that the Three D's were "how" we would accomplish our purpose. If we were going to grow in health and glorify God in the process, we needed a wider footprint. It's logical really. If we were going to reach new heights, we had to broaden our base, otherwise everything topples no matter how strong of a foundation had been laid. The pastors couldn't be expected to do all the ministry, and the people couldn't continue to pour into others as disciple-makers before they either ran dry or saturated their circles of influence. We needed more leaders.

Here's how we clarified our purpose, strategy, and measures—our "why," "how," and "what":

Why our church exists: we will help those who are far from God to become committed followers of Jesus Christ.

How we will accomplish our purpose: we will deliver the Word, disciple the believer, and deploy the church.

What we will measure for effectiveness: new believers, new groups, new leaders.

While those weren't the only things we measured, they were primary areas of strategic focus to broaden our base. We had to level the church before we could keep building. This didn't mean throwing out the solid foundation that had been built. Instead, we

> **We had to level the church before we could keep building.**

had to multiply leaders around this foundation to support the next stage of growth. If we didn't want to become the Leaning Tower of Chattanooga, we had to level the church, multiplying our ministry by giving it away. We had to rewrite a simple scorecard for measuring success in this new phase:

Number of *baptisms*	Number of *interns*
Number of people *attending*	Number of people *serving*
Number of people *in* groups	Number *of* groups

It's not revolutionary, but we needed a clear way to focus our energy. As we began focusing on baptisms, clarifying our beliefs about baptism during services and new member classes, the numbers took off—jumping the next year and more than doubling that number the following year. As we began focusing new staff members on the importance of leadership development as a step in discipleship and designated a staff person to organize an internship program, numbers shot up. As we began focusing on getting people not only into worship services, but also into volunteer roles, numbers boomed (and people who were near burnout were grateful!). As we began banging the drum again for being in community through Life Groups and launching new groups instead of adding to old ones, our number of Life Groups and leaders roughly doubled and attendance hit an all-time high!

During Jeremy's and my respective tenures at LifeWay Christian Resources in Nashville, Tennessee, former Vice President Eric Geiger hammered into us the importance of Wildly Important Goals (WIGs) from FranklinCovey's *The Four*

Disciplines of Execution.[3] Two of the starting points for identifying your WIGs were (1) that no team would focus on more than two WIGs at the same time and (2) that the battles you choose must win the war.

Our war was our mission—helping those who are far from God become committed followers of Jesus Christ. Our vision is to see one percent of the metro area worshiping with us on any given weekend. For this to happen through meaningful growth and not by gathering unhappy church shoppers from other local churches, we had to reach new people and see them developed into multiplying leaders. During Jeremy's time at Brainerd, he focused on these two WIGs:

1. Double the number of baptisms.
2. Double the number of Life Groups.

By measuring baptisms, we were identifying the first tangible step of discipleship after conversion. Measuring the number of people in D-Groups had grown nearly impossible due to the organic nature of the relationships and the gap in leadership, so we wanted to ensure we were making disciples—helping those who were far from God become committed followers of Jesus Christ. "New Christian" classes were started to explain baptism to kids, students, and their families along with general teaching on life as a disciple. The expectations of discipleship and baptism are also emphasized in our new member classes. Membership candidates are assigned to small discussion groups hosted by lay leaders while Jeremy presents big picture history, vision, and expectations. Almost without fail, people from each class choose to be baptized after discussing the significance of baptism in Christian community. For leaders, baptism is easily measured and has an exponential impact through the repeated testimony of "normal people" (as opposed to preachers) and the explanation of what it means to follow Jesus.

Second, by measuring the increased number of Life Groups, the number of leaders would have to increase by at least as many or more, since at least one coleader was expected for each group. And total attendance should increase, since a long standard rule in group ministry is that the easiest way to connect new people to groups is by starting new ones. The best way to gauge whether we were moving people along the "far from God" to "committed follower" spectrum is to get more people into and then leading groups. Out of those groups came the pools for volunteering, local ministry, and D-Groups. A word of caution that we'll expound on later, as you focus on the new: Don't neglect the existing groups and leaders. Ongoing relationships and recasting vision is essential.

Your "why," "how," and "what" don't have to be identical to ours, but you need to ensure you have clear expectations, definitions, and measures. Take a few minutes to consider the "why," "how," and "what" of your church. Be honest about your current realities and anywhere your "why," "what," and "how" aren't aligned.

Why does your church exist:

How will you accomplish your purpose:

What will you measure for effectiveness:

We want to encourage you to envision a new church—a different church, vibrant, growing church, sure. But ultimately a church where all hands are on deck.

Growing up in the church, I was constantly told that 20 percent of the people in the church did 80 percent of the work. My experience has validated that, in most cases, that isn't far from the norm. This is not a biblically faithful church and, if a church fits in that category, it is far from what God intended for the church. So what do we do about it?

Over the next few chapters, we are going to outline a pattern for you. First, we are going to explore a number of ways that our current culture—both secular and church culture—pushes back against a culture of multiplication. We can't lead the church effectively unless we understand the cultural narratives that are inhibiting biblical growth in the church.

In the last portion of the book, then, we will outline a series of biblical models that can help us chart a new direction for the church. We want this book to be both theological and practical because we believe that God is both theological and practical. We want to provide biblical, theological, and philosophical arguments that help us understand how we have arrived at the place we are at. We don't think we can rightly make the practical adjustments that are necessary apart from the biblical, theological, and philosophical understandings that have shifted. That said, we also want to offer practical steps to help you begin to see shifts in your church culture. We understand that the hardest change to see in a church is cultural change. It's far harder to change than worship styles, dress, or even the color of the carpet. And because of that, we want to encourage you that, unless God moves supernaturally, it's not likely that you'll be able to shift the culture of your church overnight. Instead, think of shifting in degrees of change. This book is intended to help you think of shifts by degrees, and in doing so, over the long haul, to help you ultimately see a church that honors Jesus and accomplishes God's purposes of helping create a biblical culture of multiplication in your church. We hope this book will help you level your church, help you multiply your ministry by giving it away.

Chapter 3

THE DANGER
OF PROFESSIONALISM

Do you remember life before streaming video services, when you actually had to watch TV commercials on cable or from over-the-air broadcasts? A few years ago, an advertisement made me laugh; I'm a bit of a sucker for humor and for baseball. A man and his wife were in a delivery room, about to experience the birth of their child. Unfortunately, no doctors were present for the occasion. Buster Posey, the legendary catcher for the San Francisco Giants, showed up, however, and offered his services to the expectant couple. Buster's argument was that, after all, he's good at catching things. The husband turned to his wife absurdly and tried to convince his wife to let the baseball legend try. The wife, of course, refused.

The commercial is a ridiculous parody, but it highlights an important part of our culture—namely, that our culture exists on an assumption and expectation of professionalism. Not only do we assume that professionals will handle the job; we also assume the professionals will stay in their own lanes, so to speak. Stick to your area of expertise. Think about it in a less surreal circumstance than the Buster Posey commercial. There was a time when most of us would've helped one another work on our cars and trucks or might have used a neighborly shadetree mechanic. But that time, with a few exceptions, is gone. We live in a time when most in our culture expect a professional, with professional certification, to accomplish most necessary services.

Our Christian lives are no different. This culture has permeated the church. When professionalism is cultivated in the same space as a culture of materialism, it can be toxic. Materialism teaches that those who attend church are the consumers, and the professional's responsibility is to deliver the religious goods and services. And often, today, we know that the religious professional is able to deliver those religious goods and services because they have the appropriate qualifications. Bible college, seminary, and sometimes doctoral degrees, not to mention licensure and ordination, are all part and parcel with the pastorate. In my experience, churches are expecting higher levels of educational attainment for those who are going to serve the church.

> **Materialism teaches that those who attend church are the consumers, and the professional's responsibility is to deliver the religious goods and services.**

It should be clear, from the beginning, that neither of us is opposed to theological education. Both Jeremy and I are in the process of earning doctoral degrees, and we have seminary degrees and undergraduates from a state university and a Bible college respectively. We love and value theological education. We choose to continue pursuing it in order to better steward and equip ourselves for the tasks the Lord has entrusted to us.

Never stop learning. Proverbs 27:17 is clear that iron sharpens iron, and one person sharpens another. Our concern is not with theological education but with the expectation that without it, we cannot rightly serve the church. This causes problems in at least two ways.

First, we have to be careful whenever we describe something as necessary. For something to be necessary in the context of the local church means that it has to be a standard for all believers everywhere. If a formal theological education is necessary, then my friends who are illiterate and poor in the bush of West Africa (where I used to be a missionary) will never be qualified to serve as a pastor. We know this is simply not the way that God intends. The Bible seems clear that the work of the Holy Spirit, God's Word, and Christian character are enough for you to be qualified to lead the church.

One of the most humbling experiences Jeremy or I have ever had was to provide theological and practical training for leaders within a church planting movement happening in a closed country. We traveled with two businessmen to consider potential partnerships, holistic development of ministry strategies, and to model for the men and women whom we met that it was not necessary to receive a paycheck or a particular education in order to be a successful and effective leader. We each took turns leading breakout classes and main sessions on everything from teaching and preaching the Bible, to deacon ministry, to basic business principles and ethics. All of these Christians faced a degree of legal, social, economic, religious, and familial pressure—and many had endured physical attacks and life-threatening persecution. While we had been blessed with education and experiences in our context, they had been blessed by joining in the suffering of Christ in their context. Grade point averages and diplomas never even crossed our minds as we met with pastors like the one who had been shot on an Easter morning and still continues to ride his bike to lead his congregation, making disciples and multiplying leaders to plant other congregations in nearby villages and other parts of the city. The cliché rang true, we were blessed at least as much or more by these faithful church leaders than they could have been by us. Where they were lacking in education, they were hungry to learn for the sake of preserving the integrity of the gospel while making disciples, developing leaders, and planting churches. Most often in our culture, education is valued primarily as a stepping stone in a career path. Go to school, graduate, get a job.

Second, we lead churches in which the vast majority of people will never have a formal theological education. We believe that they can and are being used by God in powerful ways. Being careful with this view, we must concede that a formal theological education, while imminently valuable, is not a necessary requirement for a pastor or leader to succeed. This is the moment we live in, and this moment pushes back against a culture of multiplication. When we believe that you must be a professional to serve, then the majority of our members are going to disqualify themselves because they will never have a formal theological education. This is too high a price to pay. The Bible is clear that every person is necessary and wanted in Jesus' church. Formal theological education or not, we believe that God, His Spirit, and the gospel of Jesus are sufficient provisions to allow the church to thrive.

Did you catch the word *disqualify* in the paragraph above? In church circles, the word is loaded with the moral failures of countless people we either know or know of who have disqualified themselves from positions of ministry leadership. Typically, those are clear violations of the character described in passages like Titus 1:5–9, 1 Timothy 3:1–7, and 1 Peter 5:1–4. Disqualification should come only as the result of sin. In some instances, opinions may cause conflict and therefore hinder the ability to lead within a certain context or season, but this would not disqualify someone in other contexts (see Acts 15:36–41). But notice what happens in our materialistic culture of consumers and professionals. Everyone falls neatly into one of those two categories in church—consumer or professional. Consequently, the default thinking in people's minds is not geared toward disciple-making and leadership development. It's geared toward staying in our own lanes. Professionals do the ministry for the consumers who pay them—maybe—if they like the service they're getting. With the right credentials, you're qualified; without the right ones, they aren't. They've disqualified themselves based on a cultural view, not a biblical one.

> The default thinking in people's minds is not geared toward disciple-making and leadership development. It's geared toward staying in our own lanes. Professionals do the ministry for the consumers who pay them—maybe—if they like the service they're getting.

Christians throughout the world would love to have the joy of extensive education and training, so make the most of your opportunities. But so-called laypeople like the ones we traveled with are no less capable to lead; nor are they less valuable to the church than paid staff members with seminary degrees. Theological education is a privilege not to be wasted, but it's not a necessity for ministry. This is just as true here in our Western context as it is cross-culturally.

Most likely the congregants you lead see themselves on the opposite side of an invisible (and imaginary) chasm. While they may not consider themselves consumers and may even be offended by the label at first, they probably would consider you the qualified professional. Since they earn their paychecks somewhere else and have educations in something else, they likely assume that ministry is your job and could never be theirs any more than piloting an airplane would be reasonable, no matter how many times they've traveled. They're simply along for the ride between their own jobs and the rest of their lives. As long as things are looking up, unexpected turbulence isn't too upsetting, and you have a reputation for landing on time, people are happy enough to file into their rows, take their seats, face forward, and mind their own business except for the occasional announcements and brief interactions with attendants who seek to make everyone comfortable.

I don't mean to sound cynical. I simply want to help you visualize the barrier between professionals and consumers. Are your congregants faithfully taking their seats while neither you nor they ever expect to move up and take more responsibility? Do you get frustrated that you never have enough volunteers to serve your congregation or that when a group loses a leader, people simply ask for a new one rather than a coleader assuming responsibility? What if instead of being one good pilot who flew bigger and bigger planes as he advanced in his expertise, you led a flight school and air traffic control and saw more and more pilots and copilots taking off, reaching more people and places than you could ever reach on your own? When you multiply ministry by giving it away, more people experience the joy and wonder of flying, so to speak. They realize that they can be a part of what's happening. They're no longer mere consumers; they're apprentices. You're no longer a mere professional; you're a mentor.

The majority of the people we hired while serving together at Brainerd were already committed to the church. For example, twelve staff positions on Jeremy's team were filled while he led the discipleship ministries, ten of whom were already members, and another was already committed to the church but had not yet joined officially. Only one of his twelve hires was asked to relocate for a job. Not one of his hires had completed a seminary degree when they started in their staff positions. One outside hire. No seminary degrees. Now, there were other staff surrounding these new leaders who had more education and experience. But these men and women were brought onto the team due to their reputations and character, and an affirmed sense of calling. A tremendous amount of time was spent training, coaching, and shepherding this staff on ministry leadership, theological precision, and church culture—instilling our family DNA. By the time you read this book, a few will have completed degrees and some others will have begun. But throughout that season of building our leadership base in order to level the church for future growth, we stuck by the adage of personal over professional qualifications. This didn't mean we simply looked for nice people who love Jesus. They had to fit the job requirements. We needed the right people. We prioritized character and coachability over current competence when choosing the raw material with which we believed God would build His church. Of course, related skills and experience are important, but that competency was the baseline, and the character and coachability revealed the potential.

Give me somebody highly coachable with top-notch character and foundational competence any day over somebody whose professional competence is off the charts but either their coachability or character is left wanting. Competence should increase over time with good coaching, growing together.

Pushing Back

As I said earlier, materialism can be a particularly toxic ingredient when mixed with a culture of professionalism. In an environment where the church attender is a consumer, and the church leaders are the religious professionals who dispense the religious goods and services, the consumer will believe that his or her job is simply to sit and receive while the church leader's—or, more specifically, the pastor's—job is to work and to give. "Isn't that what we pay you for?" is heard too often from church attenders to pastors about things like hospital visitation, in-home visits, and so on. Obviously, things like hospital and in-home visits are important, and I hope most pastors participate in them.

But the problem arises when we believe the pastor is the one who must do those things, regardless of whether anyone in the church participates.

This contrasts sharply with what Paul communicates in Ephesians 4. Here, pastors and church leaders are called to be equippers who train and send out the members to serve and minister in this way. This is why we have said that while the pastor ought to engage in ministry actions like visiting others, such ministry is our familial responsibility. The vocational responsibility of a pastor or church leader is, particularly, to develop the church community so we all can engage in acts of ministry together. The culture of materialism, or consumerism, that views ministry as the job of solely the pastor obviously inhibits the culture of equipping that Paul advocates for in Ephesians 4, but also leads to a truncated spirituality in the life of the believer, whom God has created to be active in ministry and for whom their spiritual growth is connected to maturing in ministry education and experience. Put simply, if believers aren't growing in their understanding of ministry and their participation in ministry, they won't grow to be like Jesus. A culture of professionalism, mixed with a culture of materialism, can greatly damage spiritual development in the life of a believer and a church.

So how do we push back against a culture of professionalism? First, we begin by affirming that getting further education and experience is good. A culture of professionalism is detrimental to the multiplication that God expects in a church. But that doesn't mean that it is wrong to gain education and experience. We affirm both of those things. But, as we have previously said, we need to ensure that we don't somehow limit ministry to those who have the advantage of formal education, in particular.

We'd encourage you to, as much as possible, make scholarships, tuition assistance, or some kind of ongoing training and education a priority for your leadership—extending the benefit beyond staff. Set up whatever criteria are reasonable for your context and encourage leaders to continually deepen their knowledge and competence. If you don't have the resources for such a benefit, be intentional about leading regular discussions of various books or articles or providing access to training videos.

Ultimately, though, we need to begin by affirming the priesthood of every believer. Scripture is clear that every believer has direct and immediate access to God and that our go-between, or Mediator, is not a pastor or a church leader but Christ. This is important because it, first, affirms that the church leader's role is not to go to God on our behalf or accomplish ministry as some sort of proxy for us. Additionally it reminds us that every believer is gifted and given the necessary ingredients to go to God on their own, and they are able to serve in ministry:

As you come to him, a living stone—rejected by people but chosen and honored by God—you yourselves, as living stones, a spiritual house, are being built to be a holy priesthood to offer spiritual sacrifices acceptable to God through Jesus Christ. (1 Peter 2:4–5)

> But you are a chosen race, a royal priesthood, a holy nation, a people for his possession, so that you may proclaim the praises of the one who called you out of darkness into his marvelous light. (1 Peter 2:9)

These remarkable verses in 1 Peter make it clear that God has gifted all believers as priests, in their own right. The responsibility of every believer is to "offer spiritual sacrifices," which implies our individual responsibility before the Lord, responsibility that we can't hand off to a pastor or church leader. Verse 9 points out that we were chosen for this task of functioning as priests in God's kingdom. This is significant. We are chosen and appointed by God to function as priests in His kingdom. This alleviates our ability to abdicate responsibility and calls each of us to take seriously our standing before Him.

Alongside this commitment to understand the priesthood of all believers, we also need to affirm the importance of minimizing the clergy-laity divide. This is tightly connected to the priesthood-of-every-believer conversation, but it continues to promote an us-and-them concept that is detrimental, theologically, but also devastates the ability of a church to create a culture of multiplication. The concept of the clergy-laity divide is rooted in a false understanding of calling, priority, and expectations. Too often we view pastors and church leaders as somehow different from the rest of the world. While it is true that God has given them a particular calling and responsibility, this is not different from any other person in the church. The responsibility may be different, but each of us in a church community has a calling and responsibility from the Lord. Church researcher Ed Stetzer reveals our unfortunate understanding in a helpful way:

> A closer look at the origin of the word "laity" reveals an issue at the root of the word itself. The word comes from a French word that comes from a Greek word that is pretty common to some of you. "Laos" was one of the first Greek words we learned, for those of us forced to study such in seminary. You know what it means? . . . "People." Now, the laity that we have made second class citizens over the years strikes back. So, if we call our non-clergy "people" I guess the clergy would be called . . . not people? You get my point, I hope.[1]

The word *laity* reveals something about how we view leadership in the church compared to how we view members in the congregation. While we view the average member as a normal person, we view the clergy as somehow different altogether. This is remedied by a proper understanding of the priesthood of every believer, among other things, but it is a necessary reality that we teach in our churches.

In John 20, Jesus is preparing to return to heaven. He has been resurrected, and He is now meeting with His disciples. After revealing to them the scars on His hands and side, Jesus commissions them to go and represent Him and His gospel. He says something that is powerful and instructive to us today as we navigate this issue: "Jesus said to them again, 'Peace to you. As the Father has sent me, I also send you.' After saying this, he breathed on them and said, 'Receive the Holy Spirit'"

(vv. 21–22). Jesus says to His disciples that they are being sent with the same power and authority that Jesus Himself had, all of which was given to Him by the Father. This drives home the point that we all are recipients of that same influential calling and authority. Jesus not only *enables* us all to be able to serve, but He *expects* us all to serve.

One reason the church is so impotent is that we are expecting a small number of religious professionals to do what God is calling the entire church to do. It's like trying to ride a bike with the handlebars, the seat, and one tire missing. It's going to hurt a lot, and you're not going to get very far. This is the church today. Jesus' call in John 20 resonates with His commission, the Great Commission, that He gives to His disciples in Matthew 28, and other passages. He reminds His followers that He has been given all authority, and He is passing that authority on to them to accomplish His task. Remember, even though His disciples were following Him, they were not religious professionals. They were fishermen, tax collectors, and the like. They were, as we read in Acts, uneducated men (4:13). In other words, they were like the average people who are members of our churches.

> **One reason the church is so impotent is that we are expecting a small number of religious professionals to do what God is calling the entire church to do.**

The book of Acts is also known by a more complete name: *The Acts of the Apostles.* I once heard someone say that it could be more appropriately titled *The Acts of the Holy Spirit.* In it,

Luke records the ongoing work of Jesus to establish the church. Acts 1:1–2 says that "all that Jesus *began* to do and teach until the day he was taken up, after he had given instructions *through* the Holy Spirit to the apostles he had chosen" (emphasis added). And look at this description from the account of the first church after Peter's sermon at Pentecost, where three thousand people believed the gospel, were baptized, and joined the church. After describing four characteristics of the community's devotion, Luke writes in Acts 2:43 that "Everyone was filled with awe, and many wonders and signs were being performed *through* the apostles" (emphasis added). *Through* the apostles, not *by* the apostles. The apostles weren't professionals or super pastors. They were ordinary men filled with the extraordinary Spirit. When the Spirit is mentioned throughout Acts, it is in relation to the proclamation of the gospel and spread of the church. It was Christ working through the church almost two thousand years ago. It must be Christ working through us today.

The key to the church accomplishing what God has called us to is the Holy Spirit of God, Himself.

We can't miss this. In order to free our churches from a culture of professionalism and materialism, and to embrace our original design of empowered multiplication, we need what those ordinary men had—the Holy Spirit. The key to the church accomplishing what God has called us to is the Holy Spirit of God, Himself.

I've spent my entire life in a theological family that doesn't talk about the Holy Spirit nearly enough. This is to our detriment. The Bible is fundamentally clear that the Holy Spirit is the person of the Trinity who equips and enables us to take Christ's gospel to the world. The Holy Spirit is the means by which every church member—educated or not, experienced or not—is able to accomplish the ministry to which God has called them. Jesus knew that we would need the Holy Spirit, and so He promised the Holy Spirit to every believer as a sign of His love for us and as the means for the believer to be able to walk faithfully with the Lord. In John 14:15–16, Jesus tells us, "If you love me, you will keep my commands. And I will ask the Father, and he will give you another Counselor to be with you forever." This promise reveals that, although many evangelicals almost seem wary of the Holy Spirit, we should be grateful for the Holy Spirit. The Spirit is God's gift to us, a sign of His affection, and He enables us to keep the commands of Jesus. Additionally, as this text reminds us, the Holy Spirit is our constant companion, never leaving us. This matters because so many seem to believe that there needs to be a supernatural experience for one to be equipped to do the kinds of things that they believe a pastor or church leader should do. This text reminds us that the Holy Spirit is always with every believer—and, therefore, every believer is always, at every moment, equipped with exactly what they need to accomplish God's purposes in their lives. And this means, unequivocally, that God expects and has enabled every believer to engage in ministry and calls pastors and church leaders to let their people loose to serve in this way, training and sending them out to serve in ministry.

Chapter 4

THE DANGER
OF MATERIALISM

I don't like shopping. When I shop, I usually get in and out of the store quickly. I know what I want and I get it. I'm also a cheap shopper. I know what I want, but I won't pay a lot of money for it. It's rare that I buy something that's not on sale. When it comes to looking for jeans, for example, I look for the best looking store that offers me the most comfortable look and fit and asks the smallest price of me. In truth, that's a materialistic approach to shopping. I am the customer, and I want what makes me happiest and costs me the least. I am shaped, in that way, by the culture around me.

Now, consider the church—or, more precisely, consider those who are looking for a new church home. What do we call people who are looking for a church, those more serious visitors who weren't dragged there by a friend or family member? We call them "church shoppers." Church shopping is the norm for people who actually want to join our churches. Too often, their approach to finding a church is almost the exact same process as my experience while shopping for jeans. Most people want the coolest looking environment that fits them most comfortably and asks of them the smallest price.

We leaders usually bemoan this reality, but I'm afraid we

are among the greatest contributors to it. We feed that materialistic environment. Without even realizing it, many of us church leaders have created or maintained materialistic church environments, all while complaining about the rampant materialism that is so prevalent in our churches. I like to call it Burger King Church. In the early 90s, Burger King ran an ad campaign that said, "Your way, right away at Burger King now." I am afraid we have created a "Your way, right away" kind of culture in the church.

Good intentions—and a little bit of ego, if we're honest—swung the pendulum of contextualization too far. A basic pastoral and missionary principle—knowing the values and vernacular of the community—became a matter of conforming to our society in an attempt to "reach people" and draw a crowd. Mission became marketing. Churches wanted to be viewed as relevant, not religious. The Great Commission of "Go make disciples of all nations" was functionally replaced with "attract a niche group of consumers."

While difficult to distinguish at times, there's a radical difference between contextualization and consumerism. Part of the distinction is motive. Are we trying to communicate the gospel and make disciples who will join the mission within our particular culture? That would be contextualization—the emphasis is on gospel ministry, advancing the mission. Are we trying to connect with more people by catering to convenience and comforts in order to share the gospel? That would be consumerism—the emphasis is on personal preferences, growth through marketing. If all we're doing as leaders is trying to inject Jesus into people's hearts in order to get them into heaven while we all continue to live according to our cultural value system, we're merely first-world syncretists. No life change is required in this case, just add belief in Jesus to your life and try to be a good person. The danger and dilution of syncretism is easy to spot in foreign contexts with pagan religions, superstitions, and shocking or inhumane customs. "How could they keep living that way while claiming to believe in Jesus?" we think as outside observers. It's harder to recognize our own tendencies from the inside of cultural norms.

It is good and right and biblical for us to contextualize so the gospel can be best understood and applied. There is an inherent danger, however, in contextualization in a materialistic culture, that we would create such a user-friendly experience that we would unburden those who are a part of the family from feeling like they have any personal investment or commitment to the church. We're tempted to treat the gospel of Jesus, or at least life as part of His church, as an add-on feature to our lives. Leadership becomes a sales pitch. We exhaust ourselves doing anything and everything we can to keep the customers coming back for more of what we can offer. No wonder our churches are so self-centered. Not only are they filled with broken and sinful human beings, but those men, women, and children are breathing the air of materialism 24 hours a day, 7 days a week, 365 days a year, even on Sundays.

Pastor, leader, we will burn ourselves out or start peddling a watered-down gospel that is nearly, if not entirely, devoid of the Living Water that really quenches the thirst of empty souls. We will find ourselves managing and marketing rather than leading on mission. None of us want to waste our lives or ministries in a state of frenzy or apathy, either of which are the inevitable result of materialistic church consumerism. No matter how much success we may achieve, something in our own heart resonates with the book of Ecclesiastes—chasing the wind. It never satisfies, at least not like we thought it would. Our congregations are filled with people who feel the same way. They come to be fed. Though they may enjoy it in the moment and feel better for a bit, the materialistic mentality of our daily lives soon has them asking, "What am I missing? What else do I need to be really satisfied?"

> Adding Jesus to our lives is actually a materialistic message. A version of Christianity where the goal is simply getting into heaven by believing and doing the right things is a gospel of syncretism—it's the American Dream plus Jesus.

The answer is not simply another update or rebranding of our churches, and certainly not of the gospel. In fact, our consumerist gospel of adding Jesus to our lives is actually a materialistic message. A version of Christianity where the goal is simply getting into heaven by believing and doing the right things is a gospel of syncretism—it's the American Dream plus Jesus. Christ didn't humble Himself in the incarnation, crucifixion, resurrection, and ascension so we could simply add that belief to our lives and get into heaven when we die. He's not an extended warranty. He's not an insurance policy. He's not an add-on. He's everything. If the gospel is true, which we believe it is, then it changes everything—including our view of leadership and church.

62

If then there is any encouragement in Christ, if any consolation of love, if any fellowship with the Spirit, if any affection and mercy, make my joy complete by thinking the same way, having the same love, united in spirit, intent on one purpose. Do nothing out of selfish ambition or conceit, but in humility consider others as more important than yourselves. Everyone should look out not only for his own interests, but also for the interests of others.

Adopt the same attitude as that of Christ Jesus, who, existing in the form of God, did not consider equality with God as something to be exploited. Instead he emptied himself by assuming the form of a servant, taking on the likeness of humanity. And when he had come as a man, he humbled himself by becoming obedient to the point of death—even to death on a cross. (Phil. 2:1–8)

Jesus' example was as stark a contrast to consumer materialism as possible. Yes, He came to save and to serve us, but He didn't cater or coddle. He modeled selflessness and sacrifice in perfect love for God. He not only *modeled* sacrifice for us, but *became* the sacrifice for us. He made salvation and new life possible. Throughout the Gospels, we read about His example and teaching, constantly correcting the cultural and religious drift toward man-made preferences and traditions, pointing out that the true issue is our hearts, not just our minds and actions. More knowledge of Scripture, belief that God was real, stricter morals, or other matters of education, discipline, and behavior modification, weren't the solution. What we love, believe, and value—the way we see life—is fundamentally broken at the core. A sinful nature is still a sinful nature whether a person is a fisherman, tax collector, centurion, or Caesar.

Jesus was not concerned with maintaining the status quo. He was not interested in drawing and keeping a crowd either. The pressure to impress, appease, entertain, and maintain our ministry responsibilities usually causes us to handle people who come to us entirely opposite of the way Jesus did.

Remember in John's gospel, after the fourth miracle where He fed the 5,000 men (plus the women and children), when people followed Him around the lake the next day, "Jesus answered, 'Truly I tell you, you are looking for me, not because you saw the signs, but because you ate the loaves and were filled'" (6:26). They were consumers. Jesus calls out their motives through one of His most challenging teachings and the result is that many of His disciples leave. It was too much for them to handle. It didn't fit into their framework. You and I would be naive to believe that we always have pure motives or that we aren't interested in keeping the crowds. It may even keep us up at night with worry, wondering whether people are going to leave.

Don't interpret this as a suggestion to intentionally run people off or that numerical growth represents compromise. Scripture is full of evidence to the contrary. Jesus also taught in the parable of the talents, for instance, that the one who is faithful will be blessed. He commanded the disciples to go make disciples, which obviously includes growth. The book of Acts, as we've seen already, is full of the explosive and exponential growth of the church. The very first gospel sermon resulted in 3,000 new converts and baptisms—an instant megachurch! But are you afraid of watching people walk away? Would you keep feeding them even if their motives weren't right in order to keep them coming back to you?

Sacrifice Instead of Shopping

This emphasis on consumer-driven environments invites the people who come to church on Sunday morning to be the crowd of consumers rather than contributors in a biblical community. An interesting New Testament passage that really helped me understand this is Romans 12:1–2:

> Therefore, brothers and sisters, in view of the mercies of God, I urge you to present your bodies as a living sacrifice, holy and pleasing to God; this is your true worship. Do not be conformed to this age, but be transformed by the renewing of your mind, so that you may discern what is the good, pleasing, and perfect will of God.

These verses are translated in different ways. This passage uses some form of the plural twice in reference to worship: "brothers and sisters," as well as "bodies." Unfortunately, some translations then translate the word "sacrifice" as a plural as well. The original language, however, indicates a singular "sacrifice." In other words, the church comes together, and the people offer their individual bodies in sacrifice, and God views our offering of worship as one singular act. Understanding the translation correctly is important to getting right the communal nature—the family relationship—of worship.

Think about the theological implication of the singular and plural nouns in the text. We are not a collection of individuals who show up on a Sunday to offer our individual acts of worship, after which we leave, although this is the popular American experience of church. We need to recognize that we are indeed a family. In many of our churches today, "brother" and "sister" are titles that we use when we cannot remember the name of the person we are shaking hands with. However humorous this may be, it's important to understand that we really are family with those who are a part of the church, those of whom we worship alongside. As a family, we come with all of our individual concerns, experiences and desires and lay all of it down at the feet of Jesus, and God views our sacrifice as one (singular) expression of worship. God calls us together as individuals, to come together under the banner of a local church where He sees not each of our own individualistic, consumer-driven sacrifices. Instead, He sees one singular sacrifice. It's the sacrifice of the local church being offered to Him. God's desire, then, is for those of us in the local church to push back against the temptation of materialism and recognize that a biblical community is a family related in covenant to one another that offers a singular offering of sacrifice to the Lord. But when we continue to cater to professionalism and consumerism, we push back against a culture of multiplication.

This kind of culture may be effective at gathering a crowd in a Western context, but it is anemic when it comes to building a multiplying culture that develops disciples and sends them out on mission to accomplish ministry. The religious consumers in this context believe it's the pastor's or church leader's job to serve their own personal needs. Their role in this religious transaction, then, is to sit back and receive the religious goods and services being offered. When a religious professional dares to suggest that it's our collective job to serve, that's asking a price that many religious consumers simply don't want to pay. That's not their job, in their mind, and they will reject it. This kind of materialistic context will destroy the multiplying church. Instead consumers believe that's what they pay the religious professionals for. What's more, even in conservative, Bible-believing churches, we have perpetuated this idea in subtle and difficult-to-identify ways.

Consider, for instance, how we classify the success of a worship service. We often judge the value of a service based on how well we have been spiritually "fed." This seems like a reasonable judgment of an effective service. We want to be in churches that value the Word of God and prioritize the right preaching of the Word, but it proves to be counter-effective in that it makes the worshiper the object of the worship service. We don't worship to get, but to give. The beauty of God-honoring worship is that the more we give in sacrificial worship, the more God fills us up. But our primary measurement tool shouldn't

> We don't worship to get, but to give. The beauty of God-honoring worship is the more we give in sacrificial worship, the more God fills us up.

be what we get but what we give. When we view worship, even with this sort of conservative materialistic worldview, we believe our job is to be filled, and it is the job of the professionals to do the filling. This leaves us with a congregation of spectators who do not view ministry as their responsibility. When God indicates clearly in Ephesians 4, among other passages, that spiritual growth is a byproduct of ministry engagement, then this spectator-focused worship service leads to truncated, immature believers.

It should not be that difficult for us to understand the importance of this in the believer's life when you consider the gospel itself. The very call to follow Jesus is a call to give up. Consider Luke 9:23–24, "Then he said to them all: 'Whoever wants to be my disciple must deny themselves and take up their cross daily and follow me. For whoever wants to save their life will lose it, but whoever loses their life for me will save it'" (NIV). This is what God is calling us to: to give up. The gospel call is fundamentally a call not to fill our life but to lay it down. When we come to Jesus, we are laying everything we are in front of Him, offering ourselves as a sacrifice. Too many Christians, however, seem to believe that the Christian life is a process of becoming the best version of themselves that they can be. This is unfortunate, but a present reality. Instead, our responsibility as church leaders is to remind the church of the call to come and die. We need to consistently repeat the refrain from Dietrich Bonhoeffer: "When Christ calls a man, he bids him come and die."[1] This call to come and die is seen in how we serve together in the church. Rather than viewing ourselves as consumers who are in church to get what we can get so we can become the best "me" possible, we come together as members of a covenant community, uniting under the banner of Jesus, working to serve for and with one another. This requires humility, it requires sacrifice. This requires the gospel.

Beyond the example of corporate worship, or even the foundational premise of the gospel, another picture that we find in Scripture that helps push back against this materialism is the concept of biblical community. While the Bible is replete with passages that push us toward biblical community, I want to pay attention to one particular passage found in Hebrews 10:24–25 (NIV):

And let us consider how we may spur one another on toward love and good deeds, not giving up meeting together, as some are in the habit of doing, but encouraging one another—and all the more as you see the Day approaching.

This passage calls us to regular gathering together as a church community. It could be easy to assume that this simply means that we all need to be together so we can worship together, but the beginning of that passage says otherwise. In verse 24, the author frames for us *why* we need to gather together: in order to push one another to "love and good deeds." This strikes us as a more intimate expectation. This call reveals an awareness of each other's lives and an intimacy with how those lives are lived. We are specifically encouraged to gather together so we can be in each other's business. This is hard to swallow in an

American context that prizes an individualistic approach to faith. This would mean that our life in the church has to be more than a once-per-week gathering for an hour of worship. This will mean, for example, investing in a Sunday school class or small group or serving in an area of ministry. Even more than those activities, though, it will mean choosing a different posture than what is typically assumed. We have to be transparent and vulnerable, which comes with risk but offers a reward worth risking for—being shaped into the image of Jesus.

> As leaders, we should not only allow but invite people into the areas of our lives that are often sectioned off into neat compartments beyond the blocks on our calendars devoted to church activities.

As leaders, we should not only allow but invite people into the areas of our lives that are often sectioned off into neat compartments beyond the blocks on our calendars devoted to church activities. There are men in my life that I (Jeremy) met in our church—peers, older, and younger—who are more than acquaintances whom I look forward to making small talk with around the coffee station outside of one of our worship venues. They're even more than members with whom I'm not embarrassed to sing around while we praise our King, to take off my shoes and get on the floor with some kids in the preschool area when it's our turn to volunteer, or to sit around the table or the living room on Tuesday nights for time in prayer, Bible study, and discussion. Beyond the scheduled routine, there are older men who will meet with me for breakfast or lunch to see how I'm doing personally and as a husband, father, and leader. They'll share from experience how they've navigated marriage, parenting, career, and even hobbies—genuinely caring about my wellbeing, not just my job performance. I invite younger guys to do the same thing, including staff and interns, in order to deepen our relationship beyond work so that holistic maturation is being fostered.

I think of the one staff member whom I hired to relocate for our Discipleship Team at Brainerd. Shaq was a young man still in school, living and working on campus at the time he was hired. He was surrounded by men at his church and school who cared for him personally. They knew that part of his childhood had been spent in the foster care system, so stability and community were especially important to him. Moving to a new state to join a new church with new people was a huge step for this young man, but he trusted the counsel of those around him to act in faith as the Lord was opening this door for him. Since the move was in December between semesters, Shaq temporarily slept in an extra bedroom in my basement until a spot opened up a week later in the church's intern house. He wasn't just a new hire to my staff; he was a guest in our home. We stayed up late on Christmas Eve putting together a foosball table from Santa. He took pictures of the kids while we all shared that Christmas morning together. Eventually, he got his own apartment, but he still occasionally comes over for dinner or to watch a football game with my family and me, to see me as a husband, father, neighbor, and friend, getting a picture of Christian life and leadership beyond what a job title and staff position can provide. Because he and I are brothers in Christ, my role was more than professional—it's personal. I want to see him grow in every way, whether it's learning to budget for a student retreat or for his own stewardship and health. Gathering together for the sake of mutual edification and growth goes beyond worship services or even work schedules—it's everyday life.

Sacrificial, let-your-guard-down, put-others-first kind of relationships aren't the norm in our consumer culture. If we have those kinds of relationships, they usually started either when we were too young to hide our mess and awkwardness, or because something traumatic happened to rip away the Sunday-best masks we hide behind and the Instagram filters we use to crop out and polish over the difficult or boring parts of our lives. There are unspoken rules of social engagement, appearance, and keeping up with the Joneses. To live the kind of life that everyone approves of—or envies, if we're being honest—requires that we have it all together and therefore need nothing or no one. We want to appear successful, carefree, living our best lives now, too blessed to be stressed. This is the game that we, our neighbors, and the people in our churches are tempted to play.

We all know the two things you don't talk about in polite conversation: religion and politics. This betrays a very privatized, personalized understanding of spiritual experiences that argues that we have business being intimately involved in this aspect of each other's lives. And yet the author of Hebrews seems to be saying the exact opposite—that we need to know one another, be invested in one another, and serve one another so we might be increasingly like Jesus.

Beyond that, consider the even stronger expectation found in the book of James, specifically 5:16 (NIV): "Therefore confess your sins to each other and pray for each other so that you may be healed. The prayer of a righteous person is powerful and effective." I've heard this verse my entire life—or, more specifically, the last half of this verse. We love the concept of praying hard and watching God work, but that's not what the verse says, does it? The verse says that, in the context of intimate community, when we lay down our facade and acknowledge our weaknesses in confession, and then the community goes to God in prayer on your behalf, God will hear that prayer and move in our lives. This is magnificent, but it is also in direct opposition to the materialistic church. In the materialistic church, those around us essentially don't matter, other than their ability to contribute to the environment that we are worshiping in. We certainly don't want to burden others with our weaknesses. After all, our worship is intended to make us stronger and better. And yet, in God's kingdom, it is the weak who are made strong. So understanding biblical community and living in transparent honesty with those who are part of your community is a vital element of combatting the materialism that kills the multiplying church.

Parts Instead of Patrons

All this leads to a church that resists the rampant materialism around us. We push back against the constant emphasis on church members as religious consumers and church leaders as religious professionals. Instead, we fight by understanding our place as a family, by embracing the gospel, and by recognizing the importance of corporate worship. And as we fight, God breaks down our barriers of selfishness and helps us recognize that what Paul said to the church in Corinth remains true today, that every person in the church is valuable and necessary:

> Instead, God has put the body together, giving greater honor to the less honorable, so that there would be no division in the body, but that the members would have the same concern for each other. So if one member suffers, all the members suffer with it; if one member is honored, all the members rejoice with it. (1 Cor. 12:24–26)

In the new member classes at our church, I (Jeremy) would always say, "If you are going to join the church, then join the church." What I would then clarify is that if people simply want to attend a worship service when it is convenient for their schedules, they were welcome to do so without any obligation to become a member of the church. Joining through membership, however, means becoming a part of the church. A line is being drawn in the sand, and by stepping across it, you are making a commitment—not just to regular attendance but to regular participation. The church is a gathering of community, not of consumers. As church members, they would be expected to participate, to serve, to give, to pray, and to be held accountable.

Contrary to the assumption of longtime members that new members were less committed, we found that raising the bar of expectation with membership resulted in more involvement, higher than our total membership averages when it came to joining regular community in Life Groups. We knew that people would respond favorably, rising to meet the expectations set before them. New members were grateful to join a church that took seriously a mutual commitment to one another. There was no pressure to join if they didn't want to get involved. People were free to worship and to attend groups and ministry events. But if they did want to serve and lead and be held accountable in community—as brothers and sisters in a faith family—then they were asked to fully commit.

Membership is a word that evokes images of a family and a body, not of a club. We are *members* of God's family. He is our heavenly Father. We are *members* of Christ's body. He is the head. As members of a club, people can demand their preferences. They're patrons, contributing financially for services and privileges. As members of a family and body, however, we set aside our preferences for the sake of health and unity. We're parts of something greater. The apostle Paul switches back and forth between the imagery of family and body, even using them both simultaneously at times (he would've been an editor's worst nightmare, mixing metaphors like this). In 1 Corinthians 12, which we

> **As members of a club, people can demand their preferences. As members of a family and body, however, we set aside our preferences for the sake of health and unity.**

touched on in the previous chapter, Paul addresses his brothers and sisters in Christ concerning spiritual gifts. He intentionally repeats the words and concepts of uniqueness and unity. Different gifts are given by one Spirit to different parts of one body at different times for one purpose. A primary point in both 1 Corinthians 12 and Ephesians 4—the latter of which contains the foundational text inspiring this book—when speaking of the body of Christ is the nature of unity, even in unique spiritual gifts and different roles of leadership. Every gift and position is given purposefully by God for the sake of the body as a whole, not for the benefit or favor of individuals parts.

Our culture emphasizes our desires as individuals. Christ unites us in selfless community. Materialism says we're all patrons and professionals in a never-ending pursuit of consuming and providing goods and services in an attempt to make ourselves happy. Christ said to deny ourselves, take up our cross, and follow Him. Professionalism says that your unique expertise serves you well and allows you to be independently valuable—and some more valuable than others. God's Word says that we share our gifts, honoring and suffering with one another, as a united body growing together to maturity. Our culture generally values uniqueness over sameness, perceiving them as contradictory. God's Word values uniqueness and sameness together, presenting them as complementary.

Let us recognize and reject the influence of materialism and professionalism that has a stranglehold on our churches. Until all members fully join together, each with their unique contributions, abilities, and gifts, our churches will never flourish. As long as we offer eternal life in heaven as the primary aim of

Christianity, our churches will never experience the abundant life of Christ empowered by the Spirit. If we keep taking up the mantle of professionalism as the paid pastor and never give ministry opportunities away, "equipping the saints for the work of ministry, to build up the body of Christ, until we all reach unity in the faith and in the knowledge of God's Son, growing into maturity with a stature measured by Christ's fullness," then we'll continue to be "little children, tossed by the waves and blown around by every wind of teaching" and trend of our culture (Eph. 4:12–13, 14). You're not the paid professional serving fickle patrons. You're gifted by the Spirit and given by God to serve the body of Christ. It's not your job to do all the ministry. It's your job to give ministry away, leveling the church so that everyone steps up to do their part.

The goal is maturity. That can't happen when professionals do the work on behalf of the patrons. Level the church. Multiply your impact. Narrow your focus. Develop others in order to give them opportunities to grow, lead, and reproduce. We are not consumers but a family of contributors who are gathered together under the banner of King Jesus to engage in ministry alongside one another, for the glory of God and the advance of the gospel.

Chapter 5

THE DANGER
OF INDEPENDENCE

Think for a minute about some of the iconic American heroes over the last few decades: classic westerns with the self-reliant John Wayne, the muscle-bound Rambo, and, more recently, the lightning-quick Jason Bourne. Each of these—while coming from different backgrounds, happening across different eras, and featuring very different storylines—shares one crucial thing in common: They are each solo heroes. They don't need anyone else. They are completely self-sufficient. They epitomize the self-made man. Think about other examples in popular American culture, like Frank Sinatra. Sinatra's iconic song is "My Way." The crux of the entire song is that he did exactly what he wanted to do in his life, and thus his life was a success. What's even more audacious is his claim, partway through the song, that acknowledges having a few regrets, but too few to mention. It's a pretty significant statement to argue that, across the breadth of his whole life, the sum total of his mistakes is almost nonexistent. We are to believe that he is, like the movie heroes above, completely self-sufficient.

The problem is, the story of self-sufficiency is ultimately a myth. There is no such thing as a self-made man or woman. But, as Americans, this is among the greatest of prizes for us.

We adore the story of the independent thinker who came from nothing, pulled himself up by his bootstraps, and succeeded. This makes sense when you consider the American ethos. There may be no more American a word than *independence*. It is the epitome of our culture. I believe the American culture today rests on twin pillars of independence and materialism. It could even be said after examining professionalism and materialism in the previous two chapters that they both lean heavily on the strength of this core idea of independence.

Professionalism can be one expression of independence: I do what I do, and it gives me unique value. I've worked hard to get where I am today, paid my dues, earned my degrees or expertise, and now deserve respect as a professional. In previous generations (like Boomers), professional accomplishments helped define a person's identity as an individual, while more recent generations (like Gen Xers and Millennials) may find more of a sense of individual identity in their professional freedom. In other words, Gen Xers and Millennials are more likely to want what they do to be an expression of who they are as opposed to it defining who they are. Consider how many of your older relatives held only a handful of jobs in their lifetime, but stuck to them for years or even decades. Certainly, advances in technology and travel, among other things, contribute to this cultural shift. But moving from job to job or even changing careers entirely is more common than not. We value independence and begin to feel limited or bored without new options or advancement. Increasingly, people are working multiple jobs or temporary jobs as freelancers or small-business owners.

Of course, those same advances in technology and travel

along with materialism and capitalism have also resulted in more business restructuring to have temporary or freelance workers instead of full-time employees. In a 2017 interview with CNN, the CEO of Intuit (which owns TurboTax, Mint, and QuickBooks) reported that "the gig economy . . . is now estimated to be about 34% of the workforce and expected to be 43% by the year 2020."[1] Meaning that there's a good chance that people reading this book already do some kind of short-term "gig"—freelance jobs, contract work, or side-hustles. (That last term doesn't have the negative connotation it once did. *Hustle* in this context means hard work, not a scam.) Individuals and corporations are both starting to value the flexibility and independence of making money without long-term commitments.

Materialism could not exist apart from independent self-centeredness. We're not talking about independence in the sense of political freedom, but the right to personal autonomy. As consumers of material possessions, we're seeking to acquire our own happiness. The spirit of materialism and independence was perfectly captured in a phrase printed on a shirt Jeremy and I saw in an airport while traveling to do some leader training. In bold block lettering, with each phrase stacked on top of the next, a man's tank top said, "I see. I want. I grind. I get." What could better summarize the current version of the American Dream? For the most part, we're free to be, to desire, to earn, and to possess anything we want. That's today's perspective on independence. Our independence is coupled with materialism. Work hard, earn money, get anything your heart desires, be happy. But that consumer worldview is not only failing to deliver on its promises, as Brian Fikkert and Kelly M. Kapic explain in their book *Becoming Whole: Why the Opposite of Poverty Isn't the American Dream*, it's destroying our churches because we've embraced this same narrative of independence and materialism.

Christian discipleship and church growth don't appear to be much different from the so-called secular world around us. While finalizing this manuscript, Fikkert shared with a group of us during a lunch hosted by the Chattanooga Institute for Faith + Work. What we knew to be true from pastoral leadership perspective he affirmed from his perspective of economic development, backed by mountains of data. It was too powerful to not include here. This toxic blend of salvation of the soul through faith in the gospel while living out our daily lives according to desires for material comforts and the belief that consumption will provide satisfaction is what he and Kapic, and others before them, call "Evangelical Gnosticism."[2] Yes, this syncretism of the gospel and an ancient heresy should be alarming and offensive. Sadly, our Bibles specifically and ironically condemn such teachings. Yet our church culture at large, with few exceptions, isn't even trying to minister holistically to develop people created in the image of God into maturity.

As leaders, what are we doing to "equip the saints for the work of ministry, for building up the body of Christ, until we all attain to the unity of the faith and the knowledge the Son of God, to mature manhood to the measure of the stature of the fullness of Christ" (Eph. 4:12–13 ESV). We aim to get people saved and to join our churches, hopefully convincing them to financially support and volunteer to serve in our churches too.

Leaders, this is not the finish line. This is the starting point. We're aiming too low, even when we're hitting our target. Again, if spiritual maturity is typically measured by daily Bible reading as individuals, and if discipleship (if it happens) is typically measured by the reproduction of sound doctrine and maybe Scripture memory, and if leadership is qualified by theological education (and perhaps business savvy for directing growth strategies and managing staff recruits), then we're functionally gnostic. We've focused our efforts on the acquisition of spiritual knowledge in the mind while disregarding the spiritual significance of daily life in the physical world. An incomplete gospel is an incorrect gospel. Salvation through believing the right things about Jesus and personal maturity coming from growing in spiritual knowledge is thus corrupted by our individualistic worldview.

> **We must avoid the human tendency to impose our cultural worldview and personal preferences onto the gospel.**

Whether reducing Christianity to spiritual knowledge that gives license to worldly indulgence or adding to Christianity through legalistic restrictions, we must avoid the human tendency to impose our cultural worldview and personal preferences onto the gospel. While converts and teachers from a Jewish background were tempted toward stricter religious observations, converts from a Gentile background were tempted toward revelry in materialistic independence. Consider Paul's letters to the churches in Ephesus and Rome, two cities dominated by hedonistic paganism and financial advantages.

Therefore, I say this and testify in the Lord: You should no longer live as the Gentiles live, in the futility of their thoughts. They are darkened in their understanding, excluded from the life of God, because of the ignorance that is in them and because of the hardness of their hearts. They became callous and gave themselves over to promiscuity for the practice of every kind of impurity with a desire for more and more.

But that is not how you came to know Christ, assuming you heard about him and were taught by him, as the truth is in Jesus, to take off your former way of life, the old self that is corrupted by deceitful desires, to be renewed in the spirit of your minds, and to put on the new self, the one created according to God's likeness in righteousness and purity of the truth. (Eph. 4:17–24)

Do not be conformed to this age, but be transformed by the renewing of your mind, so that you may discern what is the good, pleasing, and perfect will of God. (Rom. 12:2)

Drunk on Freedom

Our churches are in desperate need of renewal and recalibration. Our leadership efforts, and therefore our churches, are like cars that drift out of alignment from God's will, naturally turning inward and wayward. Our intoxicating affection for independence runs counter to Scripture and will certainly derail a culture of multiplication in the church. We're stumbling blindly in the darkness, callous from conformity to the patterns of this world. When the church is full of independent people who eschew community, mutuality, interdependence, and accountability, there is little or no atmosphere where sacrificial behavior for the benefit of the whole body can be commonplace. Multiplication dies in the cauldron of independence because, ultimately, independence is the politically correct euphemism for self-prioritization, or pride. We not only bottleneck ministry impact and effectiveness by limiting the work to professionals and leaders, but also eventually kill it off completely when it's mixed with the anti-gospel of independence.

After all, a proud and disbelieving independence was the root of sin. This distorted view of freedom and myth of autonomy leading to personal happiness and satisfaction was the very first lie to tempt human beings in the beginning. In Genesis 3, when the serpent tempted Eve in the garden as Adam appears to stand by passively, he asks her whether they're missing out on something better because God won't give it to them. If they would just take for themselves what they want, eating the forbidden fruit from the tree of knowledge of good and evil, they could obtain independence. They could know for themselves what was good and evil

Even as leaders, we have trouble believing that trusting God's Word in certain situations or under certain pressures is really best.

and therefore choose what they believed was best for themselves, without God's help or restrictions. It seems unthinkably foolish to the point of absurdity that Adam and Eve would doubt God's goodness as they experienced the joyful freedom and satisfaction of life in right relationship with God, each other, and the world around them. But we do it every day. Even as leaders, we have trouble believing that trusting God's Word in certain situations or under certain pressures is really best. So, we take matters into our own hands, relying on our limited human understanding, satisfying our own desires, justifying it with our own excuses, and bite off more than we should. We want to do it all. And sometimes our ears are being tickled by the idea that we can and should do it all. But our desire for independence—to successfully determine and achieve what's best—is a demonic lie from the pit of hell.

When did Adam and Eve experience true freedom? Joy, flourishing, intimacy, pleasure, and meaningful work were all part of life as God created it. All they had to do was trust Him, and they were free to enjoy forever an abundantly fruitful life without any worries. They were naked and unashamed. They were fully alive, completely themselves, filled with dignity and delight. Notice also that enjoying the physical world is not the same thing as materialism. Every single tree in the garden was described as being delightful to the eye and good to eat. It brings God glory to rightly behold beauty and to delight in something delicious. Our senses are part of God's very good design for men and women. This is an important distinction for us to remember in our churches. In our efforts to swing the cultural pendulum away from consumerism, we must be careful not to overcorrect. We glorify God when we appreciate His creation. Prudish asceticism does not equate holiness, and appreciation for God's creation is not synonymous with materialism. Looking to created things to provide what only our Creator can provide, however, is at the core of materialism and independence.

Independence < Interdependence

While independence is not a biblical concept—at least not a godly one—interdependence is. Both Old and New Testaments are replete with examples of how God grows His children. Consider Hebrews 10:24–25:

> And let us watch out for one another to provoke love and good works, not neglecting to gather together, as some are in the habit of doing, but encouraging each other, and all the more as you see the day approaching.

Notice the interconnected relationship between our commitment to gather with the church community and their responsibility to push us, or compel us, to "love and good works." The faith community is the primary instrument, besides Scripture and the Holy Spirit, that God uses to shape us into the image of Jesus. We need each other! That cannot be overstated.

This is hard for individualistic Americans to grapple with. Much like the trendy do-it-yourself craze—the one where we can ironically walk into big box retailers to purchase mass produced products that appear to be homemade—we have repurposed the Christian faith in a way that is generically individualistic. We claim that we don't need the church to worship, that we can worship anywhere. We claim that no one can judge us. We claim that our relationship with God is our business alone. We have even taken the process of spiritual development, and narrowed it down to an individualistic activity. The height of Christian maturity, in many American churches, is a consistent quiet time. Now, to be clear, we are not opposed to spending time with God each day in prayer and Bible study. We practice that and think you should too. But we want you to think about the fact that building an expository case for a private time of reading Scripture and possibly journaling or praying is not the easiest task, and yet the New Testament is replete with teaching that emphasizes that spiritual growth is intended to happen in community. We often seem to prefer the quiet time approach, however, because it's self-focused and we can control it.

Among conservative evangelicals, there are many who are guilty of this radical individualism in ways that are often not readily apparent. Consider how we regularly judge the success of a worship service. We leave and say things like, "That was great! I really got fed today!" This sounds mature, and faithful. It sounds like we are prioritizing good biblical teaching, but it is actually in opposition to biblical worship. When we judge the effectiveness of a worship service by what it does for us, we have made ourselves the object of the worship experience. Faithful worship is not measured by how much we are filled up, but rather by how much we are emptied out. Worship is about sacrificing ourselves in our worship of the only God who is worthy.

When I was a child, I grew up in churches where, as a

regular practice, people would come down to the altar after the sermon and kneel for prayer. This isn't as common today, but it strikes me that this should be the posture of our hearts. Our experience with God should reveal to us what in our lives doesn't measure up, and our response should be confession and repentance, being emptied out. How often do you spend time in worship and leave recognizing that there are things in your life that need to change? Just recently, I was preaching through the book of Jonah and talked about how every person struggles with biases or prejudices. The gospel calls us to recognize those problems, name them, and ask God to help us turn from them. On one hand, this shouldn't be painful—everyone struggles with bias and prejudice. And yet the realization that I am prone to bias and prejudice was painful. The beauty was, however, that acknowledging that and seeking forgiveness became an opportunity for God to apply grace in my life. In God's economy, the more we pour ourselves out, the more He fills us with the Spirit and conforms us to the image of Jesus.

Independence not only stands in stark contrast to God's design for spiritual growth through community, but also poses a tremendous barrier to a culture of multiplication. An environment that prizes the individual, and offers theological justification for that focus, will have a hard time believing that the community is primary. What's more, that individualistic focus is going to make it difficult to convince community members that they ought to sacrifice themselves for the sake of others. Every expenditure, whether money, time, or something else, has to be justified with some sort of an answer to the question, "What will it do for me?" Biblical church life is life in which the sum is more important than the parts. This is not to say that God doesn't love us or invest in us individually. Rather, it's an acknowledgment that the church is His bride, and it is for the church that He sacrificed Himself and died.

> Husbands, love your wives, just as Christ loved the church and gave himself for her to make her holy, cleansing her with the washing of water by the word. (Eph. 5:25–26)

This text from Ephesians reminds us of the depth of Jesus' love for the church and the lengths to which He went in sacrifice for her. This is our model for service in and to the church. An individualistic culture takes what should be an object of our God-directed love and turns her into a utilitarian object that exists to further our own happiness.

This consistent individualism is often the precursor to minimization of the church and even avoidance of the church altogether. Many say something like, "I love Jesus. I just don't love the church." The problem with the theology behind that kind of statement, as we have shown through the Ephesians 5 passage, is that Jesus loves the church. To love Jesus is to become like Jesus, and to love Jesus is to love that which Jesus loves. In other words, you can't love Jesus and not love the church, and to love the church like Jesus, we ought to be willing to sacrifice for the church. This lack of love for the church, and a general unwillingness to sacrifice for the benefit of those in the church, is a significant barrier to multiplication.

Instead of prioritizing a cultural norm of independence, we want to suggest that a commitment to mutual interdependence is the biblical model. God calls us to a life that is significantly intertwined with those who make up the community of faith of which we are a part. This intertwined life is a life, then, that gladly and willingly sacrifices for the benefit of those around us. Only when we embrace this mutuality will we be able to genuinely create a culture of multiplication in the church.

God calls us to a life that is significantly intertwined with those who make up the community of faith of which we are a part.

This concept of interdependence goes all the way back to the story of creation. In the beginning, God created Adam, but He did not leave Adam in isolation. This is significant because, at the time of creation, Adam was without sin and in perfect relationship with God, and yet God believed that Adam needed more. And so God created Eve. What's remarkable is not just that He created Eve, but, specifically, the reason He created her:

> Then the LORD God said, "It is not good for the man to be alone. I will make a helper corresponding to him." (Gen. 2:18)

God understood that isolation from other human contact was not the ideal, so He created a companion, a friend, a helper. Beyond that, though, God has continued to show us that the plan for humanity is that we not only be in relationship with one another but that we be dependent on one another. Consider what Paul says to the church in Corinth:

> But as it is, God has arranged each one of the parts in the body just as he wanted. And if they were all the same part, where would the body be? As it is, there are many parts, but one body. The eye cannot say to the hand, "I don't need you!" Or again, the head can't say to the feet, "I don't need you!" On the contrary, those parts of the body that are weaker are indispensable. And those parts of the body that we consider less honorable, we clothe these with greater honor, and our unrespectable parts are treated with greater respect, which our respectable parts do not need. Instead, God has put the body together, giving greater honor to the less honorable, so that there would be no division in the body, but that the members would have the same concern for each other. So if one member suffers, all the members suffer with it; if one member is honored, all the members rejoice with it. (1 Cor. 12:18–26)

God created us not only to work together but also to need each other. A church full of independent believers simply won't work—it can't work. We are to affirm the inherent value of each person in the body, we are to unite together with each member of the body, and we are to suffer and celebrate with each part of the body. There is no such thing as a faith in isolation. This imagery of a body is that of a church deeply entangled in one another's lives, and necessarily so:

> From him the whole body, fitted and knit together by every supporting ligament, promotes the growth of the body for building up itself in love by the proper working of each individual part. (Eph. 4:16)

All this is necessary because our unity is not only functionally effective, but is reflective of the character of God Himself. As the church, we must be unified and interdependent because the God we serve is unified and interdependent. I am speaking, of course, about the Trinity. We believe that God is three persons and yet one being. He is Father, Son, and Holy Spirit. And yet He is one God. One of the most beautiful passages in Scripture portraying the Trinity is found in the story of Jesus' baptism, in Matthew 3:16–17:

> When Jesus was baptized, he went up immediately from the water. The heavens suddenly opened for him, and he saw the Spirit of God descending like a dove and coming down on him. And a voice from heaven said: "This is my beloved Son, with whom I am well-pleased."

The picture here is the three persons of the Trinity, working together in concert, affirming the gospel story of God in the life of Jesus. Jesus is being baptized, while the Holy Spirit descends on Him in affirmation, and God the Father speaks His own words of affirmation, confirming their collective activity.

Hampton Keathley, the cofounder of Bible.org, has helpfully described the relationship between members of the Trinity, and our own experiences in this life:

> Since God is within himself a fellowship, it means that his moral creatures who are made in his image find fullness of life only within a fellowship. This is reflected in marriage, in the home, in society and above all in the church whose *koinonia* is built upon the fellowship of the three Persons. Christian fellowship is, therefore, the divinest thing on earth, the earthly counterpart of the divine life, as Christ indeed prayed for his followers: "That they may all be one; even as thou, Father, art in me, and I in thee, that they also may be in us" (Jn. 17:21).[3]

The picture that is present in the interdependence that God displays in the Trinity means that we ought to recognize our own interdependence. Beyond that, however, it means that we need to reorder how we understand interdependence. I think most of us might view this interdependence as a sign of weakness. In other words, if we were really strong, we wouldn't need each other. But recognizing that God Himself is an interdependent being reminds us that God, who is perfect and complete, lacking in nothing, displays this kind of relationship, thus establishing that we can be complete without being independent. In fact, I believe these texts, and others, would argue that independence is actually the sign of weakness. It is a sign that we misunderstand the nature of life and the created order and are moving away from God's good design, thus forfeiting what He has created for our benefit.

God has made us to be interconnected and interdependent. Our bent toward individualism, then, inhibits multiplication in the church, yes, but also inhibits our own spiritual growth, leading us to be less than Jesus designed us to be, leaving us unfulfilled and unsatisfied.

Chapter 6

THE DANGER OF
THE SUPER PASTOR

I have a good friend who also has years of experience as a pastor. He shared a story with me of being on vacation when he received a phone call from a deacon about an issue that had come up while he was away. The issue could have been dealt with when he returned from vacation, but the deacon insisted that the pastor return right away to deal with this specific area of stress in the church. When my friend replied, "Brother, I'm on vacation," the deacon responded, "That doesn't matter. You're still the pastor when you are on vacation." In a sense, the deacon was right, the pastor is the pastor at all times and at all places. But does that mean the deacon had a right to call the pastor to return home prematurely from his vacation?

> **Too often, church members look to the pastor to be and do what only Jesus can be and do.**

Unfortunately, that's exactly what church leaders in too many churches believe. They hired a pastor, and the pastor is always available. They probably would never admit it, but they thought they hired a Super Pastor, and the Super Pastor is always available. Too often, church members look to the pastor to be and do what only Jesus can be and do. Prolific writer and Catholic priest Henri Nouwen once wrote, "We minsters may have become so available that there is too much presence and too little absence . . . too much of us and too little of God and his Spirit."[1] Let it sink in. As pastors, our presence can become a hindrance instead of a help for our congregants' spiritual growth and health. We can "do" too much.[2]

Why should a church member wait for his or her prayer to be answered or to reach out in vulnerability to the church community when the Super Pastor is only a click away? Call. Text. Tweet. Message. Email. The church may even pay for his phone. It's his job to save the day. Churches often fail to recognize that pastors and church leaders are broken, just like church members are. They are not only broken, but finite and limited. However, I'm not convinced that inappropriate leadership expectations from church members are the biggest problem with the Super Pastor syndrome.

The Super Pastor expectations that so often seem to go hand in hand with modern church leadership are a black mark on the church. The Super Pastor is the pastor who is always on call, ready to serve. Nights, weekends, and vacations are no barrier, they never miss a hospital visit, they always preach with passion, conviction, and so on. It's exhausting, isn't it? And like many pastors, I've bad-mouthed the whole concept and bemoaned its existence. But then one day I realized that its presence was, in large part, the fuel that kept my ministry—and even worse, my soul—going. And I don't think that I am alone. I am pretty confident that the continued existence of the Super Pastor problem is the result of poor leadership from pastors even more than it is the result of bad expectations from church members.

It's easy to point our fingers at cultural influence while forgetting that we breathe the same air that everyone around us breathes. No matter what pedestal people may prop us up on or what platform we may or may not have, there's a part of our heart that likes attention. For some, the desire is easy to recognize, like a celebrity host who comically motions for more applause while telling the audience to stop. For others, it takes the loss of platform to recognize that the spotlight had become a comfort zone and even a source of identity. Most of us would probably say that we wouldn't be found at either end of the spectrum—openly craving or naively losing our identity in the role of pastor or leader—we believe we live in a healthy middle ground. But many of us live the Super Pastor story.

Many of us put on the cape and mask. Before we can move past the Super Pastor expectations of others, we have to be honest about it in ourselves. Leader after leader after leader has to struggle with this dual personality. We have a tug toward suiting up. Something inside us—something other than the call of God and work of the Spirit—wants to leave the mundane behind and be the one who saves the day. Take an honest look in the mirror and ask yourself whether you're willing to take off the mask. Is your chest puffed up, are your hands on your waist, and is your cape blowing in the wind?

What Propped Up the Super Pastor's Platform?

As former residents of Nashville who both worked in the heart of downtown, Jeremy and I were all too familiar with the spectacle of tourists on Broadway. The daily commute from our office buildings took us right through this main artery of entertainment. At any given moment, no matter what time of day or night, this route was clogged with a mixture of tourists in cowboy hats and boots, jersey-clad sports fanatics, families walking dogs and pushing strollers, symphony-goers in formal wear, screaming bachelorette parties, client meetings, and vagabond street musicians starry-eyed with the dream of being discovered. When in a good mood, the eclectic chaos was alive, buzzing with life like the assorted neon signs that lit up Broadway. It was the closest thing that Middle Tennessee could offer in resemblance to cultural epicenters like Rome or Ephesus in which New Testament churches existed. On the opposite side of the river was an NFL stadium. The Titans apparently have a long history of losing that predates Nashville by a few thousand years. In ancient Greek religion, Titans were divine beings who were overthrown by the Olympians, including Zeus, Apollo, Athena, and Artemis of the Ephesians.

When picturing the weight that Super Pastors try to carry, imagine Atlas, the mythical Titan who was doomed to stand on the western edge of the world, supporting the heavens for the rest of eternity. The difference between Atlas and Super Pastors is that Atlas was forced to carry the burden as a punishment. We (Super Pastors) voluntarily lift unrealistic expectations onto our shoulders and could put them down if we chose to. But we don't. People may expect us to bear the load ourselves, and pastoral ministry and leadership is certainly a calling, but we're in this position by choice. We have no one to blame but ourselves collectively and individually. Our cultural worldview has led to a number of ramifications in the church culture, and now we're finally at a tipping point for recognizing the massive problem that looms precariously overhead.

In chapter 3, we saw the danger of what happens when we expect professionalism by those who serve us. I don't mean that we expect professional behavior as much as I think we expect a certified professional to be the one doing the serving or work. We would never visit an unlicensed doctor, we can't show up in court with a lawyer who doesn't have a law degree, and we expect ministry to be done by professionals. In fact, when I recently had a tree cut down in my yard, I ensured that the person doing the job was insured and bonded so I wouldn't be liable for any shoddy work. This desire for professionalism coupled with a consumer-driven view of the church makes for a bad combination.[3]

As we discussed in chapter 4, most of us, I believe, shop for churches the way I like to shop for blue jeans. When I look for blue jeans, I look for the best store offering the most comfortable product and asking the smallest price from me (mostly because I'm cheap). So many of us do the same thing with the church. When we are looking for a church, we often refer to it as "church shopping." Our means of determining a good church generally center on finding a great church "product" that fits us most comfortably and asks the least of us. Once we have found a church we like, we expect a professional pastor to deliver us goods and services, of the spiritual kind. We view church as a place, not as a people, and we go there on occasion to get our spiritual "fill-up" where the professional dispenses the goods and services while we sit in the chairs, watching (many times entertained), and we put some money in the plate on occasion so that we've rightly paid for the goods and services we are receiving from the pastoral professional. We then go home, "filled up" and ready to make it through another week, as if church is a place where go to get our "spiritual pit-stop." In this environment, pastors, we aren't creating disciples; we are crafting consumers, and we are very good at it.

And in chapter 5, we saw the power of independence. Like Atlas, our cultural worldview puts each of us at the center of the universe as the axis on which the world revolves. In this context, we have built the perfect three-legged platform to elevate pastors in order to serve spiritual needs in any and all ways we deem appropriate. We've propped leaders up and in doing so we've created the Super Pastor complex. But, while many pastors decry this publicly, I'm convinced most of us never really want it to go away. It occurred to me that the churches I have served are full of people with emotional baggage. In fact, every person on the planet carries their own baggage. In the midst of this baggage, each of us tries to find ways to self-medicate to help us handle the baggage. Some use food, some use alcohol, some use sex, but we all use something. For the pastor, though, the emotional need is generally no different. We are broken just like the people in our churches. We are in need of redemption, of being put back together. And until Jesus returns, we will continue to deal with our brokenness.

> **The truth is a fair number of us use ministry as a means of self-medicating. It can be intoxicating.**

As pastors and church leaders, we have our own various kinds of emotional baggage, and while we may occasionally self-medicate using the same means as everyone else, the truth is a fair number of us use ministry as a means of self-medicating. It can be intoxicating. Pastors and church leaders suffer from identity issues, morale issues, affirmation issues, or even purpose—and each of these emotional needs are served every time a consumer-driven people calls on us to serve, and we do, and then they affirm us as the great pastor who does what no one else can do. Let's be honest, when the sweet older lady grabs us by the arm at the end of the service and says, "Pastor, no one preaches to me like you do," it's like nectar to our souls. When the couple who has been fighting calls us to their house at two o'clock in the morning and we spend the next three hours helping them navigate their crisis and on the way out the door they grab us, give us a hug, and tell us, "I don't know what we would do without you"—it is indeed sweet. But ultimately, it turns sour.

The solution to this problem is found in Ephesians 4. Paul tells the church at Ephesus,

> And he himself gave some to be apostles, some prophets, some evangelists, some pastors and teachers, equipping the saints for the work of ministry, to build up the body of Christ, until we all reach unity in the faith and in the knowledge of God's Son, growing into maturity with a stature measured by Christ's fullness. (vv. 11–13)

God's vocational design for church leaders is to equip the saints for works of ministry, not to do ministry for the saints.

> The pastor's familial responsibility is to do ministry. The pastor's vocational responsibility is to equip the members of the church so that we all can do ministry together.

In other words, we enlist, equip, and deploy the people in our churches so that, together, we serve the ministry needs of our church family. At Brainerd, we tell our pastors that we bring them on staff not to do ministry, but to equip the church to do ministry. This doesn't mean that the pastors are exempt from ministry. Instead it reframes our understanding of ministry. We contend that the pastor's familial responsibility is to do ministry. We all, pastors and members, do ministry as part of the church family. The pastor's vocational responsibility, then, is to equip the members of the church so that we all can do ministry together. We prevent anyone from taking the Super-Pastor approach when we hand off ministry, prepare others to do what we have historically done, and keep ourselves from always being front and center. Within this paradigm, pastors don't stop doing ministry. No, they do ministry but do so along with the rest of the body—and not because they are the pastor, but because they are a member of the body, and every member of the body is equipped to serve together.

The problem is that when we practically embrace a Super-Pastor model of church leadership, often in an effort to satisfy our souls that are longing for affirmation, we stunt the ability of the church to be a place of multiplication. We can't afford to hand off ministry when we need that ministry, and the applause we get because of it, to continue feeding our souls. Pastors and church leaders, we have to acknowledge our complicity in the stunting of multiplication in the church. We are often the cause of people not being developed, trained, and sent out. We are a bottleneck for multiplication and growth. Most people, including ourselves, expect the primary work of ministry to come through us.

On the other hand, we also need to remember that "the Spirit of him who raised Jesus from the dead lives in [us]" (Rom. 8:11). The same power that worked in Christ's resurrection and through the apostles at Pentecost has also been given to us. It can be said in our cities that "these men who have turned the world upside down have come here too" (Acts 17:6). So how do we unleash the potential of our churches to see a fresh movement of God?

This starts by turning our own leadership paradigm upside down. Imagine the movement and power of God being poured out through you in order to bless the people around you. The Living Water gives not only eternal but also abundant life, nurturing gospel seeds as they take root, grow to maturation and fruitfulness, and reproduce. In our current leadership paradigm of professionalism, many leaders are functioning as a funnel, distilling the grand things of God for more manageable consumption as we bottle-feed our congregations. Like temple priests, we've been the point of contact between God and the average person. People expect our presence to be like the finger of God, the tip of the funnel, providing the unique spiritual touch that people need. Ministry gets funneled through the leader to the people. The Super Pastor is in the middle, supporting all the ministry responsibilities, like Atlas on behalf of the mere mortals around him. But this isn't heroic. The Super Pastor is a myth, just like Atlas. The result is a minimal capacity for influence and impact.

Ministry
\ /
Leader
V
PEOPLE

Instead of being a bottleneck for ministry growth, we need to flip this funnel like a shower head, multiplying points of contact and ministry outlets. The surface area that we can now cover is exponentially greater. Our influence and impact increases. Now our leadership is a matter of equipping the saints for the work of ministry. We pour into them so they can pour into others. Each unique person, with his or her unique gifts, in his or her unique positions and spheres of influence can now work together to everyone's mutual benefit.

Leader
/\
People
/ \
MINISTRY

Unlike Atlas, who was doomed forever to be stuck between the heavens and the earth, you have a choice. You can step down from the pedestal you're propped up on, take off the Super-Pastor cape, and level the church. Start spreading the work of ministry around, multiplying impact by giving ministry away.

When we do this, Jesus is much more likely to get the credit. When we do everything, serving as the Super Pastor, we too easily get the credit as the one spinning all the plates. In the midst of it, we can even get more credit by appearing humble and overworked—all the while actually loving the attention and affirmation it affords to us. What might the church look like if we pushed back, in a truly countercultural way, against the rampant independence and consumerism and jettisoned the Super-Pastor approach by equipping the saints, doing ministry together, and exiting center stage? I'm convinced that Jesus would be honored. And pastor, you might just keep your ministry from ruining you while you try to use it to feed your soul.

Understand the Gospel

How do we resist the Super-Pastor syndrome? Obviously, we have to lead our churches to rightly understand what church leadership looks like, and the remainder of this book points us in that direction. But in this chapter, we need to look inward, at our own lives, and we need to consider the state of our own hearts and souls. In order for us to resist the siren song of using ministry as our own form of self-medication, our souls must first be rooted in an appropriate understanding of the gospel. God alone can satisfy and give us purpose.

Tim Keller has said that understanding our identity in Christ is significant because it is the only identity that is received rather than achieved.[4] This is no small matter. Pretty much everything else in life is based on what we can do. How large is your church? How many baptisms did you have? How much is your offering growing? These are not bad indications about a church, in and of themselves, but they are horrible assessments of your spiritual identity. In a sense it is like loving your children, and ascribing to them worth, based on how well they wash the dishes, mow the lawn, and clean their room. I don't love my children because of what they do but rather because of who they are. They are mine. In the same sense, God values us not by any effort we exert but by the gift of Jesus on the cross. That's what the gospel tells us.

One reason why so many pastors gravitate to the Super-Pastor syndrome is that so few of us are able to really rest in the accomplished work of Jesus on the cross. We run toward being the Super Pastor, subconsciously thinking we need to be, while not recognizing that the Super-Pastor syndrome is a cheap knock-off of the real thing—namely the gospel, the hope of Jesus on the cross, in your place, securing your identity, purpose, and hope. There is not one thing you can do that will secure God's love and affection for you any more than what is present right now, at this moment. That is an incredibly liberating reality.

Understand the Church

We desperately need not only to understand our identity in Christ and the gospel but also to recognize that the church is not ours. To be fair, I think we would all agree with that. The church is Jesus' body, His bride. Jesus is the head of the church. But understand that when I say that the church is not ours, I mean the church is not ours to use as some form of medication for the spiritual weaknesses that plague our souls. Not only are we not in charge of the church, but

> **The church is not created for you to use for your personal benefit.**

the church is not created for us to use for our personal benefit. This is important, because the church cannot deliver on that hope.

The church is Jesus' bride, created by God for Him. You and I, as pastors and church leaders, are given authority and responsibility, by God, to prepare His bride for Jesus, the groom. When we use the church for our own personal benefit, we are guilty of a kind of spiritual prostitution. This is dangerous territory. The bride, the body, is for Jesus. We are entrusted with a sacred responsibility to lead her and prepare her to meet her groom. She is more important, and greater, than we are. Pastor, if you believe that you are susceptible to using the church in this way (and I think nearly every Christian leader is tempted to), be honest with the Lord about it and ask Him to help you sacrificially and humbly lead the church.

Leading the church is not easy. We are called to do so with sacrifice and humility. We are also responsible for leading her with conviction and faithfulness. Getting this right is vital to leading the church to be a place where multiplication happens.

Getting this wrong can have devastating effects on not just the church but also our own lives.

Understand Your Heart

The man who came to be known as the Weeping Prophet had been set apart by God since he was in his mother's womb. It's a beautiful picture of the Lord's sovereignty and providence. The man experienced a profound calling to leadership, hearing the voice of God and then seeing two intense visions from God. But before God revealed the nature of his ministry through the visions, young Jeremiah already doubted his ability. He didn't feel skilled enough to qualify for the job. Yet the Lord chose him. But this didn't make his ministry any easier, nor more successful by earthly standards.

He earned his nickname of the Weeping Prophet through a difficult season of history and a lonely ministry. In seeing the stubborn sin of worldliness among God's people, he rebuked Judah with the harsh reality that "cursed is the person who trusts in mankind. He makes human flesh his strength" (Jer. 17:5), just like the original sin of proud independence of Adam and Eve in their effort to be like God. It's not only foolish and futile; it's cursed. While Jeremiah didn't suffer from the Super-Pastor complex, he did feel the crushing weight of despair that comes from working alone. And the people he pleaded with to come out of their worldly lifestyles were deceived into believing they were fine. After all, this was just how life was at this point; each neighbor looked alike as everyone was living out the same self-indulgent delusion. Look honestly at Jeremiah's sobering words:

> The heart is more deceitful than anything else,
> and incurable—who can understand it?
>
> I, the LORD, examine the mind,
> I test the heart
> to give to each according to his way,
> according to what his actions deserve.
> (Jer. 17:9–10)

How terrifying is the thought of the Lord judging your heart, mind, and actions? Are you drawing attention to yourself? Do you enjoy feeling needed? Is a false humility fooling everyone else but you and the Lord? Are you scared of giving away ministry? Are you insecure about developing other leaders? Are you worried that you'll be the leader to finally drop the ball and be remembered as the failure? Are you exhausted from doing everything yourself? Are you on the brink of crashing and burning as a Super Pastor?

Spend a few moments in prayerful reflection, and rest in the following prayer from the greatest leader in Israel's history —a man after God's own heart, but who was far from perfect. Despite your shortcomings and your situation, the Lord knows your heart and loves you with mercy and grace. Spend time in confession and repentance as needed. Praise God that He knows you perfectly and chose you specifically.

Lord, you have searched me and known me.
You know when I sit down and when I stand up;
you understand my thoughts from far away.
You observe my travels and my rest;
you are aware of all my ways.
Before a word is on my tongue,
you know all about it, Lord.
You have encircled me;
you have placed your hand on me.
This wondrous knowledge is beyond me.
It is lofty; I am unable to reach it.

Where can I go to escape your Spirit?
Where can I flee from your presence?
If I go up to heaven, you are there;
if I make my bed in Sheol, you are there.
If I live at the eastern horizon
or settle at the western limits,
even there your hand will lead me;
your right hand will hold on to me.
If I say, "Surely the darkness will hide me,
and the light around me will be night"—
even the darkness is not dark to you.
The night shines like the day;
darkness and light are alike to you.

For it was you who created my inward parts;
you knit me together in my mother's womb.
I will praise you because I have been remarkably and

wondrously made.
Your works are wondrous,
and I know this very well.
My bones were not hidden from you
when I was made in secret,
when I was formed in the depths of the earth.
Your eyes saw me when I was formless;
all my days were written in your book and planned
before a single one of them began.

God, how precious your thoughts are to me;
how vast their sum is!
If I counted them,
they would outnumber the grains of sand;
when I wake up, I am still with you.

God, if only you would kill the wicked—
you bloodthirsty men, stay away from me—
who invoke you deceitfully.
Your enemies swear by you falsely.
LORD, don't I hate those who hate you,
and detest those who rebel against you?
I hate them with extreme hatred;
I consider them my enemies.

Search me, God, and know my heart;
test me and know my concerns.
See if there is any offensive way in me;
lead me in the everlasting way. (Ps. 139)

Chapter 7

LEAD LIKE JESUS
Narrow Your Target and Expand Your Influence

I love when someone comes to me, or to one of our staff, with an idea for a new ministry. It's incredibly encouraging to see followers of Christ ignited with a passion for service and ministry. I often have to laugh too because so often they support their idea by saying something like, "We should do it this way because it's the way Jesus did it!" It's amazing how often we can take our preferred ministry area and convince ourselves and others that ours is the Jesus way, and that all other ways are carnal. So, the title of this chapter is not meant to tell you that this is *the* way Jesus did things and that all other ways are wrong. Instead, we want to observe some of Jesus' patterns, and we want to point out one element of His ministry in order to draw some lessons from it. We also recognize, however, that Jesus did not exclusively behave in this manner. You will understand more as we walk through the chapter.

I have often understood success like the typical American pastor. You gather believers in a church, you try to preach, sing, and lead in the best way possible, and you know it's working if more and more people start attending your church. Growing attendance equals ministry success. While this is common, I think most of us are aware that growth in attendance does not necessarily equal ministry success. I do think growing attendance can be an indicator of growth, but when I look at how Jesus invested time and attention, it's important to note that this was not the sole indicator of growth. Several chapters ago, we mentioned Jesus actually running off the crowd before  asking His twelve disciples if they wanted to leave too. We don't want to do exactly that just because Jesus did it that way in that circumstance. Jesus certainly attracted and addressed the crowds, often incredibly large crowds. But He invested the vast majority of His time and attention in developing a small group of men whom He had chosen.

We see, in Jesus' time and affection, a series of concentric circles. Of course, we could add some additional circles to indicate increasingly larger group sizes with whom He interacted or even with whom were genuinely committed disciples. For our purpose in this book and chapter, though, let's focus our attention on the group of twelve men to whom He devoted more time than He did to the public, the general crowds, or even other disciples like the 120 mentioned in the room before Pentecost (Acts 1:15), the 70 or 72 sent out in pairs to towns ahead of Jesus when the harvest was plentiful but the workers were few (Luke 10:1), or other named individuals like Mary, Martha, and Lazarus of Bethany (John 11).

By spending the majority of His time focused on a smaller and specific group of individuals, Jesus changed the whole world. We tend to operate on the reverse model. We want to expand our audience as much as possible, hoping that expanding our audience will exponentially increase our influence. Yet Jesus narrowed His focus and expanded His influence. I want to convince you that we, as church leaders, ought to do the same.

The Outer Circle

In the first circle, we find the twelve men. The Synoptic Gospels each provide a roll call for this first group (see Matt. 10:1–4; Mark 3:13–19; Luke 6:12–16). The gospel of John simply refers to "the Twelve" in a way that assumes a clear understanding of who these men were. Even if they weren't each known by name to John's audience, the importance of the group was clear. This is significant since John's gospel was potentially written from the pagan city of Ephesus several decades after Jesus' crucifixion. In each of the Gospels, the point of the group was unmistakable—this primary circle of men had a unique relationship with Jesus. These weren't His only disciples, nor were they all His most trusted friends (He knew Judas Iscariot would betray Him, for instance.) Out of His broader group of disciples, He chose twelve and named them apostles. He was intentionally developing them as leaders. This is perhaps the easiest place in Scripture to see the concept of disciple-making including leadership development for the sake of the church. Whether you want to think of them in terms of interns or staff or whatever fits your context, the point was that this was His team.

Depending on your attention span and learning style, you

may want to pause to identify your team right now before you move on to the next circle. If you'd prefer to read through the chapter before filling in each circle, then do what works best for you. What's most important though is that you don't simply move on to the next chapter without actually taking advantage of this opportunity to think strategically and specifically about how you're going to turn your own leadership paradigm upside down and start narrowing your focus in order to multiply your impact. You were called to your position of leadership by God. Your job is to equip the saints for the work of ministry. That starts by identifying your team in order to begin focusing extra time and attention on developing them as leaders.

_____

_____

_____

_____

The Middle Circle

From among the Twelve, Jesus seemed to have an even closer relationship with three specific friends—Peter, James, and John. These three men made up the middle circle. Jesus spent additional time with these trusted companions, inviting them to accompany Him in more personal moments: they witnessed the resurrection of Jairus's daughter (Mark 5:35–43), they witnessed the transfiguration (9:2–8), and they prayed until they fell asleep in the garden of Gethsemane before Jesus' arrest and crucifixion (14:32–42). This middle circle of confidants wasn't a matter of the three friends being perfect disciples. They all fell asleep repeatedly during Jesus' most intense time of need for their support in prayer. They got scared, said dumb things, lost their tempers, acted in self-interest, and scattered after His arrest. It has been suggested that these same traits that resulted in blunders and failures showed the raw material for natural leadership potential. Regardless of His reasoning, since Scripture doesn't reveal it to us, Jesus narrowed His focus even more specifically on developing these three men.

Within your own team or circle of influence, who are three people whom you can intentionally pour into on a more personal level—not just to teach them information but to model for them application, character, and experiences that they could never see otherwise, even as part of your team? If you have a specific reason for identifying any of the people, make note of it in the blank space next to their names.

_____ _____

_____ _____

_____ _____

The Center

Out of all the people with legitimate needs, genuine commitments to His ministry, curiosity about His teachings, or merely seeking His attention for other reasons, Jesus narrowed His focus from His public ministry to twelve men He would develop as leaders. From those twelve He further narrowed His focus by spending even more time personally investing in three. Finally, of course, Peter, seemed to have been Jesus' most intentional relationship. He was the clear leader among the Twelve. His name always appears first in the lists of Jesus' twelve apostles. It also appears more than any other disciple, often serving as the representative or spokesman for the group—even when he gets things wrong. For example, Peter was the only one to walk on water, even though he sank. He was the first one into the empty tomb, even though John beat him in their footrace there. He was the first to confess Jesus as the Messiah, even though he'd immediately stick his foot in his mouth by arguing with Jesus about His need to suffer and die. In the same conversation, Jesus declared that Peter's confession of Jesus as the Messiah would be the foundation on which Christ would build His church and then rebuked Satan from Peter's misguided reaction to hard teachings about His imminent death.

The three recorded instances of Jesus' more personal group comprising the middle circle were all references from the gospel of Mark, who was believed to have been someone in whom Peter invested and therefore became the primary source for the earliest gospel of Jesus' ministry. The first thing that's beautiful about this is the continued process of developing more leaders. Peter probably could have written a gospel, since two of his letters are included in our Bibles, yet his teachings were likely compiled by Mark instead. The other thing to learn from the example of the

> The Gospels don't prop the apostles up on pedestals, hiding their imperfections in order to justify their qualifications for leadership.

gospel writer and Peter (and all of the apostles in the gospel accounts) is that they don't prop themselves up on pedestals, hiding their imperfections in order to justify their qualifications for leadership. Most notably, immediately before being invited to join Jesus for prayer in the garden of Gethsemane, Peter was told that he would deny Jesus three times that very night. His most shameful moment and failure as a friend and leader was then also recorded in detail (Mark 14:66–72).

What a transformation Peter in particular would experience when Jesus sent the Spirit at Pentecost. The man Jesus saw, loved, and developed was unleashed with boldness. Only six weeks after cursing a servant girl in his repeated denials of even knowing Jesus, the leader of leaders among the Twelve was publicly preaching the first gospel sermon in the same city where Christ was crucified and three thousand people responded in faith for salvation and baptism and joined the church.

Out of the three people you identified in your middle circle of more personal mentorship, who stands out as the natural leader of leaders? What do you see in that person that is sometimes an area of weakness but is also their greatest potential strength when the Spirit is ready to use them?

———————————   ——————————————————————

Exponential Math

As a young pastor, I was mentored by a pastor who had served his church faithfully for forty years. In my mind, he was the epitome of success. During his tenure, he had led the church to grow from a small number to over four thousand in attendance every weekend. As we were meeting one day, he said something that stopped me in my tracks: "Micah, the most important thing I do each week is not preach to four-thousand-plus people. The most important thing I do is to personally invest in three men once a week, for a year." What I couldn't understand at the time, but what my pastor friend understood, is what Jesus understood: that lives are more apt to be changed up close, and that lives that are changed up close tend to have the capacity and ability to exponentially help change other lives around them. It's not that influencing large numbers of people is wrong. In fact, that ought to be the goal. We just often go about it in an unhelpful way, in my estimation. My pastor friend understood the math behind smaller groups of people. He knew that large groups of people would be influenced, likely in far more significant ways, if he invested his time in a small group and then held them accountable to do the same.

At the risk of sounding like I'm trying to sell you a Christianized version of a pyramid scheme, consider the math. It really is pretty simple. Consider if you were to invest your time and energy in 3 people for 1 year. Then, after that first year, you asked them to do the same with 3 additional people. And you each continued that annual pattern, year after year after year. The math is staggering. In year 1, you would see 3 people developed as leaders through discipleship. In year 2, you would see 9 other people discipled. By year 7, you have a megachurch discipled, with 2,187 people involved. By year 12, you have seen enough people discipled to fill up the Chattanooga metro, where I call home, with 531,441 people discipled. And by year

21, you have seen enough leaders developed through intentional discipleship to cover every location in the world. It's astonishing, really, when you think about it. One person, committed to disciple three people per year, could literally reach the world in just a few decades. And yet not only have we not reached the world in the last two decades, we have failed to reach the world in the last two millennia. Our apparent obsession with larger and bigger has often come at the expense of smaller and more intentional, the kind of focus that regularly sees lives changed and hearts transformed.

> Our apparent obsession with larger and bigger has often come at the expense of smaller and more intentional, the kind of focus that regularly sees lives changed and hearts transformed.

Focusing on Who Jesus Sees

This focus on smaller is not necessarily at the expense of the larger gatherings. After all, and as we've already indicated, Jesus spoke to the massive crowds, and did so somewhat regularly. The key here, though, is to note that this wasn't Jesus' primary practice. Jesus invested in the smaller groups, and I think one of the reasons He did so was because He understood the inherent value of each individual person. This inherent value is present because of a number of factors, but chief among them is the presence of the image of God, or the *imago Dei*, in the life of every person. God's image is part of His created order and is present in the life of every person He created. Every person not only bears His stamp of approval but also carries a representation of God Himself, a fact that affirms the value and worth of every person.

> Then God said, "Let us make man in our image, according to our likeness. They will rule the fish of the sea, the birds of the sky, the livestock, the whole earth, and the creatures that crawl on the earth."
>
> So God created man
> in his own image;
> he created him in the image of God;
> he created them male and female.
> (Gen. 1:26–27)

This presence of God's image in every person is seen in the way that Jesus showed care and concern for the most unlikely of people in His culture, people that were marginalized and unappreciated at that time including women (Luke 7:36–50), children (Matt. 19:13–15), Samaritans (John 4:1–26), lepers (Matt. 8:1–4), and so on. This extreme devotion to the individual is reflective of Jesus' love and compassion for, not to mention prioritization of, the one over the many. Jesus loved the people He was with. Jesus allowed His time and attention to be captivated by the one, or the small group, often at the expense of the larger opportunity.

This understanding of the *imago Dei* translates into how we treat everyone, of course, but even more germane to this topic, the *imago Dei* emphasizes *that* we value everyone. It reminds us that, no matter where they come from or what they have done, they are created by God for God, and their value exceeds the rest of the created order. This is, of course, among the reasons why God can call us to love our enemies and serve those who harm us. We do this not because we are masochists but because we affirm that, even when they do things against us, each person is still valued by God and capable of becoming someone who honors Him.

Maybe the greatest example of this is the apostle Paul. Now, of course, Paul was not marginalized. He came with the perfect pedigree. However, Paul's purpose in life before his conversion was to use his platform to destroy the church of Jesus Christ. He was, in many ways, the first anti-Christian terrorist. He utilized his religious platform to attack the church. God did not repay Paul in kind, however. God understood that this angry, vindictive man could become someone completely different. He called Paul, and, of course, Paul became the world's greatest evangelist. If we are going to disciple like Jesus, we are going to have to see the people the way that Jesus sees them—not as they are in the moment, but as who He created them to be.

Jesus focused not only on the individual, or the smaller group, because of His love and appreciation for the inherent value of each individual person, but on the unlikely candidates. We mentioned this briefly above, but Jesus' focus wasn't often given to those in power, or to those who were influential. Instead, He often seemed to prioritize the unlikely, the marginalized and the broken. Consider, for example, the selection of Jesus' disciples. The men He chose as a part of this inner circle were primarily men of humble means who come from unlikely circumstances, and who were not the men that most in that time would have chosen as their representatives. This is so counterintuitive to our model of leadership development today. In a culture that prizes resumes and pedigrees, Jesus went for a completely different paradigm. Even when Jesus chose someone who came with a pedigree—the apostle Paul, for example—His impact on their life led them to the conclusion that their resume was of no value (Phil. 3:3–11). Jesus understood that pedigrees and resumes were not reflective of the substance necessary for God-honoring action—humility, character, a hunger to learn, and so on.

The Un-plan

One of my favorite passages in the book of Acts comes from Acts 4:13. Peter and John are arrested for their faithful gospel preaching. They are on trial in front of Jewish leadership. The description of these disciples of Jesus is telling:

> When they observed the boldness of Peter and John and realized that they were uneducated and untrained men, they were amazed and recognized that they had been with Jesus.

These men were not the likely candidates to represent Jesus. They were "uneducated and untrained," and yet they stood out as remarkable. Why? Because it was obvious to everyone who witnessed them "that they had been with Jesus." This is exactly what happens when we adopt Jesus' model and spend time investing in the one, or the smaller group of individuals. Those whom we invest in take on the characteristics of Jesus. I am convinced that proximity, even more than plan, determines effective development in disciple-making. By that, I don't mean to disparage a plan. Plans are good. Curriculum, study guides, and reading plans can help facilitate our investment in individuals or small groups to help them become more like Jesus. But our presence is irreplaceable. We can use a plethora of different options in the discipleship process, but there is no replacement for our presence in the lives of those we are investing in.

> **Proximity, even more than plan, determines effective development in disciple-making.**

These men in Acts 4 had been in the presence of Jesus, and it's pretty clear that in the majority of their time with Jesus, He wasn't walking through a curriculum or a concerted teaching time, though those times certainly occurred. Instead, they likely spent the majority of their time with Jesus doing the kinds of things that any of us do when we are with someone else: walking, talking, learning about each other, joking around and enjoying each other's company. The key, however, was that they were in the presence of Jesus. They watched Him, they listened to Him, they learned, not just from His teaching, but from His doing and being. This experience elevated a rag-tag bunch of unlikely ambassadors and turned them into an astonishing group who gave visible evidence of having been with Jesus.

As we think about our own disciple-making, I wonder how

often we give consideration to not just *how* we disciple but *who* we disciple. Are we investing in the lives of those who are on the margins? How often are we giving our time and attention to those who might be unlikely candidates? And beyond that, how are we investing in them? Is our investment built around a curriculum and a specific plan alone, or are we creating space for us to have time together with those we are investing in? Finally, are we exclusively enamored by the large crowds, the big stage, and the bright lights? Or are we focusing on the one or the small group of potential? What matters most to us? Thinking back to my friend who pastored the seemingly successful megachurch, can we say with him, that the most significant investment we can make is in the lives of a small group of people whom we are pouring ourselves into for the purpose of developing them and sending them out to do the same?

Chapter 8

LEAD LIKE MOSES
Never Do What
You Can Delegate

A t the beginning of the book, I shared my own story of failing in a church. I mentioned, however, that taking ministry on your own shoulders and failing to share it well with others can be deceiving, because it can be "effective" in the sense that the church can grow numerically. The church can be filled with excitement. Salvation and genuine life-change can happen. But, as we mentioned in chapter 2, this assumes an incomplete scorecard. The measure of your success is not merely more people attending your church, though that's a good thing. It's not merely having an exciting church, though I believe a church that is honoring God and growing will be exciting to be a part of. A church that honors Jesus is a church that develops and disciples its members to become increasingly like Jesus, and this can't happen apart from our investment in the body, teaching them to serve in ministry.

You don't want to spend your whole life and ministry leading boldly in a way that is incomplete, and unless you pay attention, you may not ever realize that you're leading in an incomplete way. Our prayer is that this book so far has been eye-opening to the invisible undercurrents of the culture we live and lead within. Like the fish who has no idea what water is, most people simply accept life as the way things are and go with the flow. As pastors and leaders, you are probably more aware of the fact that you're swimming against the current in many ways, but we're still in the same stream. So, after identifying the cultural elements in the mix with the first half of this book, we have turned our attention toward ways to course correct with biblical examples of leadership—starting with Jesus and the Twelve. But the practice of narrowing your focus as a leader in order to multiply overall effectiveness wasn't just a New Testament or church-growth idea beginning with Jesus and the apostles.

In Exodus 18, we come across a story that will sound familiar to many church leaders. Moses was leading Israel (the original Twelve), and God was blessing them. Moses's father-in-law, Jethro, heard about what God was doing and decided to visit Moses. Upon Jethro's arrival, Moses sat down with Jethro and "recounted to his father-in-law all that the Lord had done to Pharaoh and the Egyptians for Israel's sake, all the hardships that confronted them on the way, and how the Lord rescued them" (v. 8). In contemporary terms, you might say that Moses was telling the story of God's protection and growth in his ministry. Jethro was encouraged by Moses's telling of the story, and he encouraged Moses along the way.

The next day, Moses went out to judge the people, which was part of his leadership responsibility, and the text tells us that so many people were coming that Moses spent all day and evening working at this task. Jethro then responded with astonishment: "What is this that you are doing for the people?"

(v. 14 ESV). Jethro couldn't believe that Moses was giving so much time to this particular task. Moses explained the responsibility that sat on his shoulders. Jethro, however, responded by offering practical wisdom.

I love Jethro in this story. He reminds me of what any good father-in-law should do for his son-in-law. He basically said to Moses, "What is wrong with you, son?" I laugh every time I think about this. He saw Moses working and realized that Moses wasn't working in the best possible way. Jethro doesn't just call out Moses, though. He offers him wisdom: "Now listen to me; I will give you some advice, and God be with you" (v. 19). Jethro tells Moses to create a process of delegation. He told Moses to focus on the task that only he could do. In this case, it was representing the people before God. Jethro tells Moses to choose men who can serve as able judges. Moses was to represent the people before God, he was to instruct the people and, he was to select judges. Finally, Moses was to judge the really difficult cases, but only those. The rest would be handled by the judges whom Moses had appointed.

Jethro's argument was that this would better serve Israel and allow Moses to persevere. Otherwise, Jethro understood, Moses would burn out. He would physically, mentally, or emotionally wear himself out, and then he would be no good to anyone.

Delegation, Not Abdication

There are certain things that only you can do from your position of leadership. There are innumerable things that you *can* do and maybe many of which you *want* to do. When trying to decide how to narrow your focus and multiply your impact as a leader, the questions to consider are not simply *Can I do it?* and *Do I want to do it?* If you say yes to everything you *can* do, you'll burn out and be of no value to anyone. You'll collapse with exhaustion from Super-Pastor syndrome. Jethro told Moses that he didn't have to do everything he was capable of doing. Other people could also be capable of taking on certain tasks. Hanging on to those things is bad leadership. On the other hand, passing off everything that you simply don't want to do is also bad leadership. You may need to be the one to do something that you don't like to do. Being the leader doesn't mean you get to choose the perks and enjoyable tasks and send the other stuff down the ladder to the folks who haven't paid their dues yet.

If your typical practice of so-called delegation is essentially to ask people to do things you don't like or want to do, then you're likely not delegating. You're abdicating. You're shirking responsibility for convenience and comfort (a sign of independence and consumerism). Healthy delegation seeks a solution. Unhealthy delegation deflects a problem. Avoidance and apathy toward responsibilities that are unpleasant or difficult is not a perk of climbing to the top of the ladder. Making ministry assignments based on those criteria could be cowardice or laziness. It can be ego and a celebrity mentality rather than a shepherd mentality (a sign of

> **Healthy delegation seeks a solution. Unhealthy delegation deflects a problem.**

professionalism). Your job is to do what you need to do for the sake of your church. What is healthiest for those you lead? At times, what will be healthiest for everyone is doing something yourself. Other times, you come to a point where for your own health, and therefore for the sake of those you lead, you either need a break or start delegating for the sake of multiplication.

When it comes to focusing your attention and multiplying your impact as a leader, you have to ask yourself the following questions. Notice that there's always an actionable step based on the answer to a simple yes or no question.

DELEGATION FOR MULTIPLICATION

Something needs to be done.

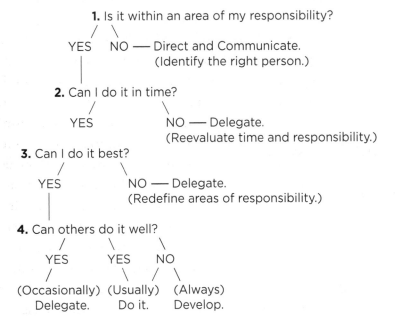

Step 1: Is It within My Area of Responsibility?

As soon as you're aware of a need as a leader, your first step is to identify the person responsible for meeting that need. If someone else has already been developed to a point of overseeing the responsibilities for that area of need, you direct attention to that person and clearly communicate what you've observed. At that point, your primary work is complete, and you are freed to focus on your unique area of responsibility.

A good example at Brainerd is with respect to our missions efforts. Like most pastors, I get a lot of phone calls and questions from people who want our church to partner with them. Because I also have a particular passion for missions, I get contacted a lot for such reasons. In our leadership structure, we have a team that is responsible for our missions strategy. When I am contacted, the best thing I can do is not meet with the potential partner. Instead, I direct them to our missions team. This both allows them to work in their gifting and calling, and frees me to devote time to the things that I am specifically tasked with.

Step 2: Can I Do It in Time?

If a particular task falls within your area of responsibility as a leader, the next question to ask is purely pragmatic. Realistically, do you have the bandwidth to meet this need in a timely manner? If you can't perform a task within the necessary timeframe, you need to delegate the responsibility to someone who can. But your responsibility doesn't end in this case with simply assigning the task to someone else. You also need to reevaluate your time. Why didn't you have the ability to meet a need that was within your area of leadership? Certainly, this will occur on occasion. Life happens. Opportunities present themselves. Tragedy strikes. But if you're constantly in a state where you have too much to do and not enough time, you're a point of bottleneck for ministry effectiveness. Your time restraints are limiting the growth of your ministry and the health of your church. So, either your time management needs to drastically improve or you need to reevaluate your area of responsibility, considering the likelihood that it's too big and that the Super-Pastor syndrome is going to run you or your ministry into the ground—or both. You need someone to help you carry the load before it's too late. Your process of evaluation should include ways to begin sharing the load until someone else is ready to take it off your shoulders completely.

Recently, I had a project that needed to be completed by a deadline. It required a fair amount of research. I knew that I would have to spend significant time studying if I was to handle the project well. I also knew, though, that I was under the gun with respect to the deadline. I have a young guy who is starting out in ministry who works with me. I realized that I could ask him to help me compile research. It would help him grow in the discipline of research, and it would help me by sorting through a lot of content and putting research in front of me so that all I had to do was spend time studying rather than spending a long time finding the research and then studying it. In this scenario, I knew I couldn't hand off the entire project but, for the sake of time, I knew there were portions of the project that I could hand off, and it would make for a better project, and it would help a young guy become more effective in his field.

Step 3: Can I Do It Best?

When you have time to do something that is within your area of responsibility, there's another question to ask. This question is a strategic one that requires even more humility than the second step about evaluating your time. Just like you don't want to overextend or overcommit yourself, spreading yourself so thin that you don't have anything of substance to offer, you likewise don't want to keep doing something that someone else who has the time could do better. If you truly want what is best for your church, then you'll be willing to delegate responsibilities that you may even enjoy to someone who has more bandwidth or ability to do the job well. When something pops up that you know would actually be a great fit for someone else on your team, delegate that opportunity to them. If they're constantly better suited for a certain task, consider redefining your areas of responsibility to allow them to become the go-to leader for meeting those needs that play to their strengths.

If you feel a twinge of insecurity pricking at your ego, be assured that not only will the body benefit by repositioning each of you to focus on your strengths, but you also will gain credibility and loyalty as a leader by entrusting honorable responsibilities to gifted members of the body. Your job isn't to do the ministry but to equip each person to play the part that best serves everyone. You're becoming a leader of leaders in this instance. An area where I really struggle is with respect to detail, specifically in the area of finances. I recognized a long time ago that this part of our church's ministry is better handled by someone else. At Brainerd, we had to go through an extended time when we did not have a permanent person overseeing this area of our church's ministry. Instead, I watched over it while a number of other staff members primarily carried the load. Even though we had great staff members handling various responsibilities, my role providing ultimate oversight was not helpful or effective, as it should be. The best thing I could do as a leader is to hand this off to someone else.

Step 4: Can Others Do It Well?

Finally, when everyone is positioned to do their best work, and you're serious about delegation for the sake of multiplication, you have one final question to ask. In the previous steps, there were more cut and dried answers, even if they took a humbling gut check. Step 4 is more a matter of discernment and intentionality for the sake of your mission in the long run. You could technically stop at Step 3 and you would have successfully directed and delegated responsibilities; you would have reevaluated time management and even redefined leadership roles to maximize giftedness. At this point, you should be at peak performance.

But the goal isn't optimization. It's multiplication. Growing to full maturity means bearing fruit—continually—and multiplying. Step 4 is what takes your leadership to the next level. This is where the most intentional multiplication occurs.

In this final step, you've already determined that you are the best person for the job. Don't miss the significance of that. This step is huge. Was Moses the best judge among the twelve tribes of Israel? Absolutely. Jethro recommended an evaluation of time and a redefinition of responsibilities in order to focus Moses's energy on only what was absolutely and uniquely necessary. But eventually even Moses wouldn't be there to make the hardest decisions and to lead the people. Getting through Step 3 puts everyone in their healthiest position for their current circumstances. Step 4 prepares everyone to move into the future.

As the leader best equipped to perform a certain task, you still have three action steps. If nobody else can do what you do well, it's time to start developing leaders in this area. In this case, you usually perform this task, but you should always be developing new people too. (This may even be where your middle circle of three people from chapter 7 comes into play.) What are you doing to intentionally help new leaders grow into the unique ability that you are so good at? For example, as a preacher, do you ever share the pulpit and do anything to raise up new preachers? I don't just mean when you're out of town. Developing new leaders means being present to help them grow. Not only are you not able to give the same kind of coaching and feedback, but if others only lead in your absence, it subtly communicates to them and to your church that they are of less importance. So, as you develop other leaders, it's important that you occasionally delegate opportunities that they can

> As you develop other leaders, it's important that you occasionally delegate opportunities that they can handle well, even if you can handle them better.

handle well, even if you can handle them better.

As long as you continue taking these steps, your overall trend line should be upward, seeing growth over the years in maturity and fruitfulness. If you don't delegate opportunities for the sake of multiplication and developing future leaders, any momentum you gain even through the first three steps ends with you. One way we do this at Brainerd is through team sermon preparation. Sermon prep is one of the most important things a pastor does. I can't hand it off completely, but I recognize that it is done better in community. Our sermon prep is almost never done in isolation. We meet annually as a team of five to ten people to plan out our sermon series for the upcoming year, and then we meet weekly as a group to evaluate the text and identify the main point of the text and the outline of the sermon. Once that is done, that gets put into an online shareable document, and the group collaborates together all week on the sermon outline/manuscript. The end result is a much better product than if I were working alone, and I'm also developing others in the art of study and sermon development. While this is not an area that I will ever completely hand off, it is an area where others can share the load—and in doing so, our sermons are better and others are developed.

Bonus Question (*The Step behind the Steps*)

Another question to consider that is not as cut and dried as the others identified for healthy delegation is the question *Am I expected to do it?* Meeting expectations is a delicate balancing act for leaders. By definition, *leading* is about progress, which requires moving people out of their comfort zones. If you aren't meeting expectations, people will eventually stop following, even if they are willing to do so for a while purely out of respect for the position of leadership. Eventually, your credibility is shot—whether or not the expectations were clear or fair. People eventually make up their minds to stop following, and you may not even have been aware of these unmet expectations. Even if most people are still following, if key people stop following, it will eventually lead to an unhealthy situation.

For example, our church had grown accustomed to hearing the previous pastor mention "discipleship." On one hand, this made my (Jeremy's) job of Discipleship Pastor easier. But on the other hand, it created some challenges. As Micah's passion for missions became increasingly clear, certain people began to wonder whether we were no longer "about" discipleship. We had to constantly reconnect the dots that discipleship and mission had always been intertwined biblically and even in our church strategy—Deliver, Disciple, Deploy. This was true not only from the pulpit but also from within my own areas of emphasis. One of my tasks was to reemphasize and integrate Life Groups alongside D-Groups. Again, both had previously existed, but the D-Group environment had been emphasized to the point that Life Groups began to feel unvalued and wondered what their place was in ministry. Now, as Life Groups received more attention, D-Groups and their advocates felt less important. Because the language and personalities had shifted, expectations felt unmet at times.

The powerful dynamic of expectations also proved to be especially true in an established church that had experienced recent growth. Although no church is truly the same generation after generation, since the vast majority of people will change, our church has been meeting for ninety years on the same street corner. It's vital for new staff (like ourselves) to understand not only what the current policies, procedures, and programs are, but also what the previous practices have been. I found that even though the majority of the people I was leading had been members for less than eight years, I was attempting to lead members who had been around for decades. Even changes made under the previous pastor still felt "new" to them. No matter how long your church has existed, people will have certain expectations of ministry programs, church governance, and even attitudes and opinions to be held by leaders. Even in a church plant or young ministry, people bring expectations from past experiences. Taking the time to understand these dynamics will be an investment worth making—it may be invaluable to the current and future success of your ministry.

The key to this step behind the steps, so to speak, is constant and clear communication about expectations and intentions. A feedback loop is critical. Leaders have to continually cast vision about where their churches are headed and clarify the steps that are being taken to keep them moving in that direction.

Challenges to Multiplication

When we think of multiplying ministries—ministries in which God is clearly working—we often think about the good parts of it, but we can forget the difficulty. Leadership has to adjust and modify as ministry expands and grows. We can't be who we used to be. This is difficult for us leaders. But if the ministry is about God, and not about us, we have to be willing to adjust our leadership to meet the demands of the ministry that God is growing around us. This is, simply put, what leadership stewardship looks like.

What makes it so difficult to hand off ministry responsibilities? There are a number of reasons, but among the most significant is the myth of self-sufficiency. "I can handle this," we often say. We think it even more often. The problem with that kind of thinking is that, even if we can accomplish a task on our own, our responsibility as church leaders is not simply to "do" ministry. We are responsible to equip the saints for ministry. So, often, when we accomplish tasks, believing we are getting things done, we may actually be failing to get done what we are called to do.

Self-sufficiency is rooted in a misunderstanding of our own capacity and goodness. It ignores the inherent weakness and sinfulness that each of us struggles with. Self-sufficiency is, at its foundation, a form of atheism, assuming that we are not in need of anything and that we can captain our own ship. The problem is, first, that Scripture denies this. Beyond that, though, our experience in life undermines this idea. There is no such thing as the self-made man. An old Nigerian proverb says, "It takes a village to raise a child." Dhati Lewis has revised that saying in a way that I think is helpful: "If it takes a village to raise a child, it takes a church to raise a Christian."[1] We see this truth throughout God's Word. And yet we push back against it. We do that because, going all the way back to Adam and Eve in the garden of Eden, we are tempted to believe that we don't need God or anything else. The serpent tempted Eve by asking,

"Did God actually say . . . ?" (Gen. 3:1). He was attempting to elevate Eve's confidence in herself, and he was eroding her confidence in God and His Word. He would go on to question God's motives, saying, "In fact, God knows that when you eat it your eyes will be opened and you will be like God, knowing good and evil" (v. 5). He was trying to convince Eve that she didn't need God or His directions; she needed to trust herself. In today's vernacular, we might say that Eve needed to "believe her truth." This obvious attempt to circumvent objective truth in favor of subjective experience ended up in disaster, of course, not only for Adam and Eve but also for every person who came after them, including you and me. We all are guilty of continuing the sin of Adam and Eve, and we continue to fall prey to its penalty. We believe we are enough, and when we pursue the route of self-sufficiency, we fail. Moses was failing, and Jethro, thankfully, offered him a kind corrective that ultimately helped save both Moses and all Israel.

Self-sufficiency is a temptation for every pastor. We worry that if we hand off responsibility, then we'll be out of a job. Or that people will think we are lazy. Or that people will think we are bad at what we do. Almost all those concerns are rooted in how we think others will perceive us.

> We need to understand that handing off ministry is both God's design for our leadership, and the means by which our leadership may be made to last.

We are fearful of man and not respectful of God's expectations. So, we need to fight self-sufficiency. We need to resist the temptation to do it all ourselves. We need to understand that handing off ministry is both God's design for our leadership, and the means by which our leadership may be made to last. God is good to us in that way.

Leading in Isolation

This story of Moses holds an important lesson for us that should shape the way we think about leading in ministry. Notice that Moses did not explicitly seek wise counsel but that Jethro gave it to him anyway. It is difficult to overstate the significance of wise counsel to those of us who are in leadership. Far too often, the assumption of self-sufficiency is birthed in the isolation of church leadership. Leaders are often lonely. This is obviously bad for the leader's mental and emotional health, but it is equally bad for the health of the church body. In their book *Pastors at Risk*, H. B. London and Neil Wiseman relate some data from a study conducted by the Fuller Institute of Church Growth.[2] Among the findings that they share is that 70 percent of pastors say that they do not have someone they would consider a close friend. Unfortunately, this is a trend that seems to be increasing across the country. According to a 2015 *Time* magazine article,[3] the number of Americans who say they do not have a close friend has tripled in the last few decades. When asked how many confidants they have, "Zero" is the most common response. We are an increasingly lonely culture, and pastors seem to be leading the way. So, when you combine our loneliness with a propensity towards self-sufficiency, you get a toxic combination of poor leadership decisions. God under-stood this from the beginning. It's, in part, why He said, "It is not good that the man should be alone" (Gen. 2:18 ESV). It's also why we read in Proverbs 15:22, "Plans fail when there is no counsel, but with many advisers they succeed." We need the counsel of others. What's maybe most ironic about Jethro's advice is that the one that all of Israel was coming to for wisdom and counsel was, arguably, the person in the nation that was most in need of wisdom and counsel. This is precisely the pain that the church leader so often feels.

All this loneliness, and the need for counsel, undergirding a philosophy of handing off ministry means that pastors and church leaders have to work to develop the skill to hand off ministry. The beauty of this responsibility is that it transcends church sizes. In fact, I think smaller churches may actually have the advantage here. This is true because we're not just talking about delegating and handing off ministry; we're talking about delegating ministry and handing it off to those who are not employed as pastors/staff members in the church. The impor-tance here, going back to Ephesians 4, is that those who are in official church leadership are called to equip the body. As we see in the example of Jethro and Moses, one of the ways that we can do that is to enlist, train, and hand off ministry to those around us. In order to effectively accomplish that, we need to work at developing the skill of delegating. Because this obvi-ously does not come naturally to us as we pursue self-sufficient leadership, it will require shaping and developing.

Delegating Authority, Not Just Responsibility

One of the most challenging aspects of delegation is the distribution of responsibility, authority, and affirmation. When we delegate, we have to distribute responsibility. In other words, we are asking someone else to assume a specific responsibility. We are saying to them, "This is your job now." This is, frankly, probably the easiest part of delegation. A bit harder, but vitally necessary, is the importance of handing off authority to accompany that responsibility. If we are going to expect that others will accomplish tasks, we also have to extend to them the necessary authority to get it done. This can be challenging because handing off authority can feel, even more than handing off responsibility, as if we are losing something. In our culture, authority often equals value and position. It seems counterintuitive to give it away. And yet this is exactly what we see Jesus doing in Luke 9–10, when He sends out the disciples. They go out with both His authority and the responsibility that He extends to them. They come back to Him, then, celebrating what God accomplished through them. Consider the words of Luke 9:1–2: "Summoning the Twelve, he gave them power and authority over all the demons and to heal diseases. Then he sent them to proclaim the kingdom of God and to heal the sick." But then, most importantly, we hand off not just authority and responsibility but also credit. This, as we addressed in chapter 6, can be among the most difficult of things for a pastor or church leader to give up. When we understand church authority rightly and recognize that God is the head of the church and the one to whom all glory is due, this should not be difficult. But, unfortunately, too many pastors and church leaders thrive on the credit that is extended to them for the work they accomplish. When this is the case, handing off the credit can be devastating to our well-being, and so we resist.

One of the first things I did when I arrived at Brainerd was work to develop a preaching team. We used a combination of live preaching and video preaching, and we were moving toward a multisite model that would require live teaching, and so I knew that we would need to develop a team of skilled preacher-teachers. This solution would create a more diffused ministry model, but it would also mean that I would be preaching to fewer people each week, and it would also mean that I would have to risk people believing that I wasn't necessarily the best preacher at our church. All of that was nerve-racking for me, to be honest. We are currently in the process of developing our next campus, as a matter of fact, and we have identified the person on our staff who will be the campus pastor and who will preach every week at this new campus. He is an incredibly gifted preacher and, if I'm honest, I've had moments when I've worried that he might grow a campus larger than the campus where I preach. My struggle with my own insecurity whispers that it would be a blow to my ego for him and for that campus to succeed. It's an internal struggle but one that I think is worth dealing with. The potential for a diffused ministry that advances on multiple fronts is far too significant in comparison to a single-focused ministry that rises and falls on the back of a single individual.

The answer to so much of this, though, is rightly placing

God at the head of the church and the one to whom the glory is due. The church is in need of a renaissance of humble leadership who seek to push themselves out of the spotlight and direct the credit to God. We need to recapture the words of Psalm 115:1: "Not to us, LORD, not to us, but to your name give glory because of your faithful love, because of your truth." When the pastor and church leaders have rightly established God as the one who is worthy of our praise, God as the head of the church, and God as the only one to whom credit is due, our pride can be eliminated from the equation. This transfer of credit, then, can lead us to a place where delegation is not a scary proposition, but one that frees us to hand off ministry, accomplishing what God has called us to do as we equip the saints for the work of ministry.

Chapter 9

LEAD LIKE PAUL
Model and Mentor

I have trained for a long time to be a pastor. I have multiple degrees from theological institutions. I have mentors who have invested in me and helped develop me. But, in many ways, the most formative pastoral training I have received came between the ages of twelve and eighteen. In those years my dad served as a small church, bivocational pastor, and I tagged along. When my dad would officiate a funeral or a wedding, I would tag along. When my dad would visit someone in the hospital or in their home, I would tag along. When I preached my first sermon, at seventeen years old, it was my dad who helped me write it. There is no single, formative ministry influence in my life that is more significant than my dad. What's more, my personality is just like my dad's. I am a product of my dad's genes and also of his influence. Having a loving father is one of God's good gifts to many of us, but having a loving father who is also a pastor is a godsend for anyone serving in pastoral ministry themselves. What made this time with my dad so formative was not the lessons he intentionally taught me, to be honest. It was, instead, the opportunity to participate in a bit of an observational ministry laboratory.

In my family, we are Green Bay Packers fans. My dad is from Wisconsin, and although I've never lived in Wisconsin, since the time I was a very young child, my dad taught me to cheer for the Green & Gold. We say, "Go Pack Go," a lot around our house. Since I married my wife and became a father to three kids, we have thoroughly indoctrinated all of them. Now, this life-long fascination and dedication to the Packers is thorough, but not one time did my dad sit down with me, curriculum in hand, to teach me about the history of the Packers or the great players in Packers history. No, I just grew up with a dad who loved the Packers, who surrounded us with Packers memorabilia, and who watched Packers games, with me, all the time. I learned to love the Packers, and then I picked up the rest on my own from either being around and watching my dad or studying the Packers because of my inherited love for them.

Ministry has been much the same for me. To be fair, I have studied ministry at great length. I have studied the Bible. I have studied theology. I have studied church leadership. I have studied church history. However, most of my study is the overflow of a love for God and the ministry that my dad imparted into my life in a young age. A good example of this would be the wedding ceremony that I use today. When I perform a wedding, I use the same basic wedding sermon that I have been using for nearly two decades. I obviously modify it based on the couple I'm working with, but it's essentially the same. And it's not even mine. This sermon is one my dad helped me put together about twenty years ago when I performed my first wedding ceremony. Both the content of the wedding ceremony and the form it is conveyed in are a reflection of my dad, his ministry, and his passion, and all of that has been passed down to me. I am still working to be like him.

This is exactly the kind of ministry model that I want us to consider in this chapter. Specifically, I want us to consider the example of the apostle Paul with Timothy, a man whom Paul referred to as his son in the faith and someone whom Paul invested in as a leader in training. Paul's intentions with Timothy were obviously driven by his affection for him, but they were also obviously driven by his desire for Timothy to develop into a great leader.

To Timothy, my true son in the faith. (1 Tim. 1:2)

There are plenty of discipleship models in the New Testament, and many of them revolve around leaders who intentionally use their gifts to develop others around them who will become leaders themselves. But, from my view, there may be a no more beautiful example than the picture of Paul and Timothy. It is a picture that is much closer than a simple discipleship relationship. This is highly relational, deeply intentional, and rooted in love for one another. I fear that this kind of relationship is often missing in the church. How often are our relationships simply transactional instead of transformational? Relationship, intentionality, and deep concern for one another drives this kind of transformational experience that transcends an educational transaction.

Proximity > Plan

Inevitably, when I teach on this topic and implore people to invest, personally and relationally, in the lives of those coming behind them, I am asked, "What curriculum do you use?" In fact, without fail, it's the single most often-asked question that I get. It's not surprising, really. We live in a culture that thrives on schedules, curricula, and plans.

> *That* we are together is of even greater importance than *what* we do together.

We live in a Western culture. But if I can offer a bold suggestion, when it comes to a mentoring relationship that looks like Paul and Timothy's relationship, proximity matters more than plan. *That* we are together is of even greater importance than *what* we do together.

This is difficult for us in a Western culture. We want to divide our mentoring time into blocks or periods of time. We want to maximize that time to learn as much as possible, and then we want to move on to the next item because accomplishment is among our highest virtues. And yet, when you consider Paul's relationship with Timothy, or the disciples' relationship with Jesus, for that matter, it appears that they had far more time simply being together than they had in some form of official educational moments. The vast majority of Paul's influence on Timothy, and Jesus' influence on the disciples, would almost certainly have come through more relaxed relational time as they traveled together and served together. This should not surprise us, though, as this is the experience that most of us know and appreciate. Whether it's the experience of a parent, a grandparent, or a friend, those who usually have the greatest influence on the way we live and work and play are those with whom the greatest amount of our time with is relational and casual, rather than formal and planned.

Now, that does not negate the idea of using a plan. I love plans, and I use them. In a moment, I will share what I most often do in modeling and mentoring, but my larger point here is to encourage you that transformational relationships require extended periods of time together, in relational settings. For me, this means that my wife and I open our home for meals, to watch sports, or to talk and answer questions. This happens, usually, multiple times each month with people we are investing in. Beyond that, it also means that I rarely travel without taking someone with me that I am investing in. Whether it's a conference, a speaking engagement, or some other opportunity, I try to take someone else with me who can spend time with me, and whom I can invest in relationally.

This pattern and priority of proximity is validated by the life of the disciples, especially in the book of Acts. We read one particular story of how God used the disciples in front of the Sanhedrin, the religious court for the Jewish people. The Sanhedrin were angry with them, but Peter and John were able to testify to the goodness of God in Jesus. And the response of the Sanhedrin is so telling, as we noted back in chapter 7:

When they saw the courage of Peter and John and realized that they were unschooled, ordinary men, they

were astonished and they took note that these men had
been with Jesus. (4:13 NIV)

Notice that language. *These men had been with Jesus.* It was
their time in the presence of Jesus that shaped the way they
engaged the world.

Having established the importance of proximity over plan,
let's not eliminate the idea of an actual plan. I utilize a plan,
but I try to keep it simple. I usually try to determine up front
the amount of time I am going to spend with the ones I'm
investing in, and then we divide
our time between studying a book
of the Bible and then studying a
popular book on a topic that's appropriate for their age or stage in
life. When we gather to meet, we
spend half our time studying the
content for that meeting, and half
of our time talking about their
walk with the Lord, areas of personal struggle, and their family. I
also leave some time, as much as possible, for questions and
answers about anything they are interested in.

> Leadership development was part of their discipleship. The relationship was one of mentorship, not just education.

This process of organic intentionality—prioritizing proxim-
ity over and above a rigid plan—is, I believe, closest to New
Testament leadership development methods of Paul with Timo-
thy or Jesus with the Twelve, or especially with Peter, James, and
John. Leadership development was part of their discipleship.
The relationship was one of mentorship, not just education.

Lifestyle Mentoring

So what prevents us from practicing this kind of lifestyle of mentoring? First among our obstacles (or excuses) is our unwillingness to dedicate this kind of time, not to mention the transparency necessary to open our lives to constant scrutiny when we share our lives over extended periods of time together. As Westerners, the issue of time is a particularly challenging one. Everything we do revolves around a timed schedule, and as a result, we regiment nearly everything. Because we are regimented by time, and because we are so accomplishment-oriented, we believe that each object in front of us is an opportunity to maximize time, and then we must move on so that we can use the extra time productively.

This is a constant challenge for me. Since I became the pastor at Brainerd, I have averaged approximately fifteen to twenty meetings per week, and that is with only four office days per week. As I am writing this, it's a holiday, and this week we have one less workday and my schedule has fourteen meetings on it. I literally have to block out extended time to study and to spend time with people I want to develop. If I do not, my schedule will overwhelm me, and I will never have time for investing in others. I also know that one of the ways that I can redeem time is to invite others to be with me, even when I don't necessarily have anything planned. This past week, one of the young guys I've been investing in called me and asked if we could get together. He's recently started a new job, and it's been harder for us to meet. I invited him over on Sunday afternoon after worship, and he hung out with us. We talked, ate lunch, and then I took a nap while he played with my son. Times like this can be an opportunity to invest relationally and intentionally (through conversation), just by making time to be in proximity with one another. We often fail to see that this kind of relational time investment is, in fact, a productive opportunity. As long as we continue to repeat phrases like, "Time is money," and the like, we will find it difficult to invest larger periods of time. We will think of each discipleship or developmental moment as a scheduled activity that needs to be accomplished and then moved on from. This will consistently inhibit our ability to be able to fully invest, relationally, to the degree that the mentor relationship that we see in Paul's and Timothy's lives might develop.

George G. Robinson perfectly gets to the heart of informal mentoring and intentional discipleship: "You don't have to add *something* else to your calendar to mentor or disciple someone, you simply have to add *someone* else to what's already on your calendar."[1] This is the simplest and most natural thing on earth, inviting people to be with us in our daily routines. Yet we genuinely convince ourselves that we're too busy or unqualified to mentor or disciple someone else. Not only do Jeremy and I do this as a regular part of our lives (not just our jobs), but our wives do too. In addition to meeting with young women, especially college students or recent graduates, for more formal discipleship on a certain night of the week, they'll also invite them along to attend a kid's sporting event, to join a workout, or to share a meal. We make time for these things already. Why not add someone to the experience?

You may be surprised at how meaningful it is to be included in part of someone else's personal life. Meeting with someone to study a workbook for a few months can be great, but joining one's family for a hike through the woods and throwing hammocks up between a couple of trees for lunch could be something they'll never forget. Experiences not only add to learning ability and deepen relationships; they're enjoyable! They'll see you living out your life, making decisions with your spouse, laughing with your kids, being patient when the car won't start. Over time, all sorts of conversations will naturally arise, and the one you invite into your schedule will become increasingly comfortable around you and will open up to you and trust you with something they truly need help with.

Beyond making time, though, there is the tremendous challenge of opening our *lives* up to one another, especially to those that we might want to invest in who are younger than we are. We have to make ourselves vulnerable too. Being genuine and honest is an important start, but too many relationships (even with discipleship) stop with authenticity if they even get that far beyond head knowledge and surface pleasantries. To be vulnerable requires a deeper level of trust. I can be authentic while still guarding myself and being in control of the relationship. Vulnerability levels the relationship out. In a culture where we want to always appear confident and convey the idea that we are in

> I can be authentic while still guarding myself and being in control of the relationship. Vulnerability levels the relationship out.

charge at all times, it is difficult to allow our idiosyncrasies, or our weaknesses, to be on display.

Not long ago, I traveled to our annual, national denominational meeting. I took a young man who we were developing and who now serves on our church staff. While we were there, I realized that I was in the process of passing a kidney stone. I have passed quite a few of these, and so I knew that it would not be enjoyable. What complicated things was that I was sharing a hotel room with this young man. Unfortunately, as the pain increased and my body responded violently, this young guy had to see me in my most vulnerable, pained, and weak state. It was not a pretty sight. He was kind to me, and he worked to help me as he could. These kinds of experiences are not ones we are accustomed to sharing with others outside of our immediate family and maybe very close friends. This is tragic, truthfully, and not just because of the loss of pragmatic benefits that I believe come from sharing our lives with those whom we are trying to invest in and develop. No, this is tragic because it misses the mark of how God's Word describes biblical community.

Many of us love James 5:16: "The prayer of a righteous person is powerful and effective" (NIV). It's a beautiful verse. But that's not all of the verse. I had almost never, if ever, heard the entire verse until I was well into adulthood. Consider what the rest of the verse says: "Therefore confess your sins to each other and pray for each other so that you may be healed. The prayer of a righteous person is powerful and effective" (NIV). Yes, the strong prayers of those who are with Jesus are powerful. But notice the context within which these powerful prayers are offered. Those who are transparent enough to confess their sins to those who are close to them can experience God's power moving on their behalf as their friends go to God in fervent prayer on behalf of those who are in need. This is a far cry from the common interpretation of the verse that seems to simply say, "Pray hard enough, and God will move."

Take the Initiative

So, what should we do about this? In short, be the initiator. If you are a pastor, or a church leader, then you can develop someone else. Even if you are young, or feel inexperienced, there will be someone who is coming along behind you; someone who can be your son in the faith, if you will. In my experience, young adults are longing for mentors, for relationships with those who are more experienced and who can provide wisdom and guidance. Also in my experience, most of those who are older are glad, or even convicted, that they ought to develop those who are coming behind them. I am convinced, then, that the invitation to this kind of relationship, generally speaking, should come from the more mature individual. Those of us who are a little further along ought to actively look for those whom we can invest in, and then we ought to be the ones extending the invitation. In fact, this very evening, as I was partially done writing this chapter, I was reaching out to some folks about my own intern/mentor process for this coming school year. There is a pretty good picture of this in the New Testament in the life of Jesus:

As Jesus was walking beside the Sea of Galilee, He saw two brothers, Simon called Peter and his brother Andrew. They were casting a net into the lake, for they were fishermen. "Come, follow me," Jesus said, "and I will send you out to fish for people." At once they left their nets and followed him. Going on from there, he saw two other brothers, James son of Zebedee and his brother John. They were in a boat with their father Zebedee, preparing their nets. Jesus called them, and immediately they left the boat and their father and followed him. (Matt. 4:18–22 NIV)

The picture of Jesus, in this text, is that of the one who is more mature (obviously) reaching out to those whom He wants to be His disciples. He went to them and called them, and they left what they were doing and joined Him for the next three years. We must be like Jesus and Paul and countless others, and take the initiative to reach out to and invite those who are coming behind us to join us, in our lives, to learn together with us and then ultimately to be sent out as servants of Jesus.

While I think it is primarily the responsibility of the one who is more mature to reach out to the one who is less mature, it is not wrong for those of you who want to be developed to reach out to someone more mature. This has been my pattern at a number of points. I am unashamedly hungry for more mentors, and I gladly ask for wisdom every chance I get. In my past, that has translated into something as long as a multi-year mentoring relationship, and something as short as a meal where I came prepared with a notebook and a pen, and asked plenty of questions and took copious notes. Don't be afraid. If you aren't being pursued for a relationship like this, be willing to pursue it yourself.

Finally, take the one you are investing in, your Timothy, if you will, and do mission and ministry with that person. The laboratory is the best place to watch and experience learning from those who are more mature than we are. And beyond that, it's important to note that Jesus' own call to His disciples revolved around mission. Consider how Jesus called the very first disciples, as we saw above, in Matthew 4. He called them to be His disciples and promised them that they would become fishers of men. Then consider Jesus' very last words in the Great Commission, found in Matthew 28. He tells His disciples to go and make disciples. It is no small thing, in my mind, that Jesus originated and culminated His relationship with His disciples around the concept of mission. Don't miss the key and significant opportunity to invest in others, specifically as we join together in ministry and mission. We see in the examples of both Paul and Jesus that discipleship was leadership development. The maturation process wasn't complete until multiplication was taking place. As a pastor or ministry leader, be sure that you don't stop short in your process of discipleship. You are uniquely called and equipped to mentor and multiply new leaders.

Chapter 10

LEAD LIKE TIMOTHY
Train and Deploy

*You, therefore, my son, be strong in the grace that is
in Christ Jesus. What you have heard from me in
the presence of many witnesses, commit to faithful
men who will be able to teach others also.*
—2 Timothy 2:1–2

In this short passage from Paul's letter to his son in the faith,
Timothy, Paul gives Timothy instructions for how he is to
pass on the gospel, how he is to develop leaders, and how he is
to bless the church. Specifically, Paul implores Timothy to take
to the study of Scripture, theology, ministry lessons, and more,
and to have a plan for passing them on to those who would
come behind him. The background for this specific book of the
Bible is important. Paul is writing to his son in the faith who has
been pastoring the church at Ephesus. Paul is asking Timothy to
make the church ground zero for theological education.

This is consistent with the New Testament's emphasis on
the centrality of the local church. A survey of the New Testament will quickly reveal to us that the local church is the locus
of God's kingdom activity on earth. The pinnacle of God's activity on earth is rooted in the local church. This is true not

only practically but also theologically, as the church is that which Jesus died for and is His bride, for whom He is returning. Understanding, rightly, the primary place of the church helps us understand the importance of the church as the center of theological education and development. Over the years, we have created theological institutions of higher learning. These institutes, colleges, universities, and seminaries are tremendous blessings as they come alongside the church. However, I am convinced that the local church is primary in the process of developing those within the church body theologically.

You may remember that the previous chapter emphasized relational proximity as more important than a rigorous plan when it comes to mentoring. This is where solid curricula and more structured plans come into play. This process of theological education, as Paul commends to Timothy, should serve to develop the leaders who will continue to invest in and help lead your church. But it should also serve to develop the laypeople in your church. Thomas Jefferson once wrote that a well-informed electorate is a prerequisite to democracy. If I could extend his quote a bit, I would argue that a well-informed congregation is a prerequisite for a healthy, growing church. We have to know the truth in order to lovingly obey and grow in Christlikeness. We can't rightly relate to one another as the body of Christ if we all aren't growing in Christlikeness.

> Build up the body of Christ, until we all reach unity in the faith and in the knowledge of God's Son, growing into maturity with a stature measured by Christ's fullness. Then we will no longer be little children, tossed by

the waves and blown around by every wind of teaching, by human cunning with cleverness in the techniques of deceit. (Eph. 4:12–14)

Can all your people recognize false teaching? I know every person in my own church can't. That's not a criticism. That's not even a confession. That's just the reality. Scroll through the social-media feeds of church members and see what they post, share, tweet, and like. If something were to happen to you or to any of your leaders, would your area of ministry responsibility recognize whether the next person to preach, teach, or lead started heading in a new direction theologically? The truth is you and I won't be in our positions of leadership forever. We need to equip everyone in our churches, not just the person who happens to be on the platform, to believe God's Word. I pray our churches will be like the Bereans who double-checked even the apostle Paul's theology!

> If something were to happen to you or to any of your leaders, would your area of ministry responsibility recognize whether the next person to preach, teach, or lead started heading in a new direction theologically?

The people here were of more noble character than those in Thessalonica, since they received the word with eagerness and examined the Scriptures daily to see if these things were so. Consequently, many of them believed, including a number of the prominent Greek women as well as men. (Acts 17:11–12)

Word of G.O.D.

According to the American Bible Society, roughly 90 percent of households in the United States own a Bible, which is great news. A recent survey shows that only 20 percent of Americans claim to have actually read the Bible in its entirety. Among men and women who self-identify as Protestant, which would include the congregation Jeremy and I serve, about 39 percent report daily Bible reading, even though most pastors include reminders about the value of personal reading in their sermons, offer free Bibles to members and visitors, and even provide some sort of suggested reading plan.[1] The question we have to ask ourselves as leaders is not whether we are providing access to the Bible or even whether we're emphasizing the importance of reading the Bible. The question isn't even do people have a starting point on "what" to read. Rather, the question seems to be do people know *how* to read the Bible? Do our people know what to do with it once they crack it open?

There are numerous methods for studying the Bible and learning theology. As someone who has worked for multiple publishers and with countless pastors, authors, and churches of various denominations, I (Jeremy) have seen that there are strengths and limitations to just about any plan. But as someone who has been writing curricula for over a decade now, I'm also a firm believer that any plan is better than no plan when it comes to theological education and leadership development. Content is important. Contextualization is essential. What worked in one church, denomination, region, or decade may or may not work in your own setting.[2] First, let me share a generic tool for Bible study that everyone in your church can utilize. Then we'll get into more formal training ideas.

> **Content is important. Contextualization is essential.**

While serving as a college pastor in my early 30s, I recognized that I needed a simple and reproducible tool for equipping college students to not only lead and multiply small groups on their campuses, but also instill a basic discipline of Bible study and disciple-making. My worship pastor at the time worked with church planting movements in North Africa and the Middle East, and the transformative nature of obedience-based discipleship that he told me about had sparked a fire in my heart to rethink the basic approach to ministry that I had grown up with and been using as a student pastor before that. Convinced of the truth Paul wrote to his young protégé in 2 Timothy 3:16–17, I developed and implemented an acronym that distills a simplified form of inductive Bible study and obedience-based discipleship models similar to church planting movements among communities with few-to-no believers. At Brainerd, we have implemented this acronym in every age group, including the family worship guides as drive-home questions for parents to ask their children about the sermon from that morning.

WORD

- What verses are you studying?
- How would you summarize the main point of this text?
  - » Who wrote it? To whom did they write it? Why did they write it? What do you know about the original cultural context?

G—God

- What do these verses reveal about *God* (or especially about the Father, Son, and/or Holy Spirit)?
  - » All of God's Word is His self-revelation. How can we get to know Him better by what is said directly or indirectly, explicitly or implicitly?

O—Ourselves

- What do these verses reveal about *ourselves* (and others—humanity)?
  - » We don't need to read ourselves into the text, but what does it say about the human condition? Or what thoughts and feelings did you experience?

D—Do

- What should we do in response to these verses?
- Identify specific actions and reactions to the text.
  - » Are any commands or clear principles given in the text?
  - » Application should be specific when active responses are identified, otherwise accountability

and growth becomes theoretical rather than practical and actual.

» Not all of Scripture is intended to have a specific application; sometimes the response may be more affective—awe, praise, humility, love, or conviction. Emotional responses are appropriate, but if we identify only emotions and knowledge whenever we read Scripture, then we are not truly applying the Word of God.

The order of these four points is vital to a healthy understanding of Scripture. The first thing anyone should do when studying the Bible, other than to pray for the Spirit to enable us to hear from God in order to know Him better, is to make note of the broader context and purpose of the passage being read. Why was the book of the Bible written and what is the purpose of this part of the book or letter? Keeping the overall message in mind provides a framework for properly understanding and applying God's Word, preventing a "what this means to me" perspective that strays away from the truth and possibly even into heresy. As a leader, provide recommendations for a good study Bible, online tools, and commentaries as helpful resources in these important details.

Once they've identified the main message of the text, people must learn to read Scripture in order to see God as primary. The Bible is God-breathed as His self-revelation. It is first and foremost about Him, not us. So before people in your churches can know what God is saying to them and how to appropriately respond, they must know who He is. Next they must be honest about what Scripture is revealing about their own hearts. You've likely heard the pastoral adaptation of a quote from the Poet W. H. Auden: "A real book is not one that we read, but one that reads us." And finally, once we've seen God for who He is and let His word reveal who we are, people can rightly respond in worship and obedience. Without this final step, people are merely engaged in devotional inspiration or academic exercise. Identifying a response enables account-ability in community and encourages growth in maturity.

Training

After providing a foundational discipline of self-feeding on the Word of God, how then do you move your people on to the solid food of rich doctrines? For the purposes of this chapter, in keeping with our general theme of the book, I want to en-courage you to develop a theological training process in your church. Certainly this includes discipleship courses, as is often typical in churches, but it ought to also include something of more depth and substance than is often the case. How are you developing and teaching your people theology, missiology, ec-clesiology, eschatology, and so on?

The good news is that many local educational spaces such as institutes, colleges, universities, and seminaries have recog-nized both the importance of local church-based theological education, as well as the potential of increasing their student base, and they have made partnership with local churches much easier, allowing churches to not only train and develop their people, but also allow their members to progress in formal theological education, sometimes even making possible under-graduate and graduate degrees that can be offered through a combination, of classes taught by church staff at the church, online education, and other flexible options. Brainerd has part-nered with a theological institution to do something like this, which not only has served our people but also has the potential of even greater things in the future.

One of the beauties of prioritizing local church-based theo-logical education is the lasting power of this kind of process. In an era when traditional institutes, colleges, universities, and seminaries are often struggling with declining enrollment, in-creased costs, and other challenges, the local church stands out as an example of staying power. As J. T. English has pointed out, connecting theological education to the local church lends spiritual vitality to the process: "We know that the church will withstand even the gates of hell, and so we know that if theo-logical education happens in the local church, disciples will always be made."[3] I love English's point here. When we recon-nect things like theological education with the church, we are acknowledging the spiritual stability of Jesus' church. We are affirming that these processes can withstand time and spiritual attack because of God's design and plan for the church.

Beyond all this, though, we also need to affirm that the model many of us have been using has not worked well. We have arrived at a time when our churches are filled with theo-logically ignorant, or at least theologically anemic, members. A recent study conducted by LifeWay Research in partnership with Ligonier Ministries found terrifying results concerning the theological awareness, or lack thereof, of American evangelicals. Consider these, among their findings:[4]

- 66 percent of American evangelicals agree that everyone sins a little, but most people are good by nature
- 51 percent of American evangelicals agree that God accepts the worship of all religions, including Christianity, Judaism, and Islam
- 54 percent of American evangelicals agree that God counts a person as righteous not because of one's works but only because of one's faith in Jesus Christ

There are a host of other statistical pieces that will frighten you about the state of the church, but these small examples provided above underscore the very real spiritual and theological poverty that we face in evangelicalism. We need a serious recommitment to theological development in the local church, and we cannot simply depend on other institutions to do that work for us. Sending our folks off to them can be beneficial, but is far too limited in scope and, frankly, is guilty of handing off the church's responsibility. We have to do something different.

> We need a serious recommitment to theological development in the local church, and we cannot simply depend on other institutions to do that work for us.

In order for us to take advantage of this opportunity and to recapture the biblical model of church-based theological education, we are going to have to reshape our pastoral priorities. This takes time. It takes investment. The average pastor that I know does not have much time and often feels worn out with little left to invest. The only way we can successfully navigate this transition is for our leaders and people to understand the importance of making this change, and then allow for a reprioritization of responsibilities to make it happen. The beauty and synergy of this need is that when we begin to put into practice the principles throughout the rest of this book, we develop a well-trained and equipped church capable of standing in the gap and taking on some of the responsibilities so the pastor can heighten and prioritize the church's investment in theological education.

This process will also require, truthfully, many pastors to redouble their efforts to strengthen and invest in their own theological education, making sure that they are not guilty of embracing a watered-down theology in their own life. And as the pastor and leaders commit themselves to more robust theology, they will be better able to pour into and develop their own people. This is in keeping with Paul's affirmations to Timothy later:

> I solemnly charge you before God and Christ Jesus, who is going to judge the living and the dead, and because of his appearing and his kingdom: Preach the word; be ready in season and out of season; rebuke, correct, and encourage with great patience and teaching. For the time will come when people will not tolerate sound doctrine, but according to their own desires, will multiply teachers for themselves because they have

an itch to hear what they want to hear. They will turn away from hearing the truth and will turn aside to myths. But as for you, exercise self-control in everything, endure hardship, do the work of an evangelist, fulfill your ministry. (2 Tim. 4:1–5)

Those of us who pastor are called to this end. We are called to prepare, we are called to be ready, and we are called to do all of this as a part of our pastoral responsibility. Paul understood that this would be important specifically because of theological impotence among the people and the constant tension of theological compromise. All of this should lead us to a place where we not only emphasize training and development in the church but, going back to Paul's words to Timothy in 2 Timothy 2:1–2, anticipate that this process leads to raising up our pastors and leaders from within the church as the dominant model of leadership development. The model we see used so frequently today is that lay leaders and deacons are raised up from within the congregation, but that pastors and paid leaders are often hired from outside the congregation. It is true that the New Testament shows us examples of this kind of process.

Consider Timothy. Timothy was pastoring the church at Ephesus, and yet he was from Lystra in what is central Turkey today. Lystra was a long way from Ephesus. Timothy wasn't from Ephesus and wasn't raised up from within that church. Timothy pastored the church even though he was sent to the church from somewhere else. There are certainly other examples. So, to bring a pastor or leader in from the outside is not wrong. I am pastoring a church that I was not a part of prior to becoming her pastor. However, while it's not wrong for this to occur, I am convinced that the New Testament teaches a framework in which the majority of our leadership, including pastors, is raised up from within the congregation. Titus, for instance, was sent by Paul to lead the churches on the island of Crete. Paul instructs Titus, however, to appoint elders in each of the churches across the island. The picture here is that Titus has come from the outside, but is expected to identify and raise up leaders from within the congregation to step in and assume these key leadership roles.

This kind of thinking will require retraining in most of our churches. In most of our churches—going back to the culture of professionalism that we discussed in chapter 3—many if not most of our people feel like they are unqualified. Truthfully, because the church has done a poor job developing leaders theologically and practically, it may be the case that many of them are not, in fact, qualified at this point. We have to adjust and employ a better process. So our investment in leveling the church, in tearing down the clergy/laity divide, and in creating a culture where people are equipped and empowered to serve has to become a higher priority.

> Our investment in leveling the church, in tearing down the clergy/laity divide, and in creating a culture where people are equipped and empowered to serve has to become a higher priority.

At Brainerd we try to accomplish this, in part, through the creation of something that we call The Brainerd Institute.

We fashion it as something of an academic exercise, with eight weeks semesters, two in the fall and two in the spring. We offer them as simple courses for laypeople in our church to take if they want to expand their understanding of theology, hermeneutics, teaching, missions, and more. We also have partnered with a national seminary to make these classes available to people who want to earn seminary credit at the undergraduate and graduate levels. We have a certificate track for people who simply want to gain more knowledge and aren't looking for a degree, or they can go the degree route and gain credit through the seminary while we teach the classes in Chattanooga.

This process allows us to accomplish a number of things. First, it helps us better train our members so they are on level ground with our pastoral staff in terms of theological training. Second, it allows us to root theological training in the local church, rather than having to send our young adults off to an institution, allowing us to both better train those in our church and be more likely to keep them as a part of our church in the long run.

Chapter 11

MAINTAIN
OR MULTIPLY

I (Jeremy) will never forget my dad's words of counsel as I accepted the role of Discipleship Pastor, knowing the foundation that had already been laid: "God isn't putting you into a position of leadership to maintain what has been but rather to move it forward." This is true for each of us. Ultimately, we all will stand before King Jesus. I will. You will. Every staff member, church member, and volunteer we've ever collectively led will stand before King Jesus. On that day, what greater joy could be imagined than hearing these words:

> "Well done, good and faithful servant! You were faithful over a few things; I will put you in charge of many things. Share your master's joy." (Matt. 25:23)

You know this parable from Matthew 25. We all have been entrusted with different churches of different sizes in different places, made up of different people with different gifts. But we've also been entrusted with the same gospel, the same Spirit, the same mission.

So what will you do with what He has entrusted to you? Will you cling tightly to it, scared to risk anything beyond your control happening to His church? Or will you do whatever you can with whatever you have to make much of Christ to the glory of God? Will you trust the goodness of your King, investing wisely to multiply what you've been given?

I don't want to stand before the Master, white-knuckled, only to say that I've managed not to lose what He gave me.

I don't want that to be any of our testimonies: We didn't lose it, God! It's still here!

We have a gospel mission to accomplish and local churches to lead. We have a responsibility to lead in such a way that is faithful to the Word not only through preaching, teaching, and singing, but also through modeling, ministering, and multiplying.

> Pay careful attention, then, to how you live—not as unwise people but as wise—making the most of the time, because the days are evil. So don't be foolish, but understand what the Lord's will is. (Eph. 5:15–17)

Imagine what might happen if we made the investment to rethink our shared identity as a church and our responsibilities as leaders. What if leadership development was part of our discipleship and everyone started doing their part—and found joy in it!

> Therefore I, the prisoner in the Lord, urge you to live worthy of the calling you have received, with all humility and gentleness, with patience, bearing with one another in love, making every effort to keep the unity of

the Spirit through the bond of peace. There is one body and one Spirit—just as you were called to one hope at your calling—one Lord, one faith, one baptism, one God and Father of all, who is above all and through all and in all. . . .

And he himself gave some to be apostles, some prophets, some evangelists, some pastors and teachers, equipping the saints for the work of ministry, to build up the body of Christ, until we all reach unity in the faith and in the knowledge of God's Son, growing into maturity with a stature measured by Christ's fullness. Then we will no longer be little children, tossed by the waves and blown around by every wind of teaching, by human cunning with cleverness in the techniques of deceit. But speaking the truth in love, let us grow in every way into him who is the head—Christ. From him the whole body, fitted and knit together by every supporting ligament, promotes the growth of the body for building up itself in love by the proper working of each individual part. (Eph. 4:1–6, 11–16)

What if we informally but intentionally invested like Jesus, Moses, Paul, and Timothy? What might happen if we tore down the walls of professionalism, materialism, and independence, leveling our churches in such a way that the Super Pastor could stop trying to do everything and start sharing the burdens and joys of ministry with others around him? We believe that if we flip our paradigm upside down, leadership influence and ministry effectiveness wouldn't keep bottlenecking with the staff, and we'd see a fresh movement of the Spirit unleashed through our people.

It feels risky or like wishful thinking, but it's perfectly logical and thoroughly biblical. This dream of what the church can be drives us to continually reevaluate our own methods and motives. But no matter when we've had success (legitimate or perceived), when we've failed (which is plenty), or when we've been hurt (ministry is messy), we aim to keep learning, keep moving forward, and keep our focus on seeing the local church growing in health, maturity, unity, and fruitfulness.

> **We believe that if we flip our paradigm upside down, leadership influence and ministry effectiveness wouldn't keep bottlenecking with the staff, and we'd see a fresh movement of the Spirit unleashed through our people.**

The confident belief that the church is the bride of Jesus, and that she is worth all the effort, drives us. The love for the church drives us. We believe that there is a better church ahead for those who take seriously this biblical expectation. Until Jesus returns it won't be a perfect church, but a better church is ahead.

We have spent the past decade or more working toward this end. It has caused tension and pain at points, as we have to help our people rethink pastoral responsibilities and the roles of the church member. But, as halting as our steps have been at times, when we look at the churches we have served, we see people who have stepped into leadership roles who might never have thought themselves able before. We see churches strengthened and thriving, even in the absence of a pastor, because people have assumed leadership responsibilities. We look across the country and see pastors and leaders whom we have invested in serving the church and leading groups to know and love Jesus. More than anything, we see people who are looking increasingly like Jesus.

I (Micah) told you at the outset that I had failed. The truth is that I still fail. Not in the way that I originally had failed. But I still fail. As much as I believe what we have written in this book, I still get it wrong at times. There are times when I don't emphasize the basic truth of this book as much as I need to. My ego gets in the way or I fall back into old habits or I struggle with bad pastoral expectations. Over the years I have learned that this does not happen without significant intentionality and hard work. There are too many factors in the American church pushing against this biblical model. It does not come easily. So I have failed from time to time, but as I keep walking with Jesus, I see Him strengthening me more and more. The church is a messy place, and our lives as leaders are certainly messy as well. But in the midst of this mess, Jesus is working, shaping me, shaping the leaders around me, and shaping His church. And in that mess, His work is beautiful. In this mess, He is leveling His church, making her into His beautiful bride. If you commit to seeing God level the church you serve, you are going to fail too. In those moments, you have to lean into grace and remember that Jesus is the one who builds His church, using broken leaders like yourself.

One of my favorite passages of Scripture, and a text that

inspires me, is Colossians 1:28–29. Paul speaks about his own motivation to love and serve the church:

> We proclaim him, warning and teaching everyone with all wisdom, so that we may present everyone mature in Christ. I labor for this, striving with his strength that works powerfully in me.

Creating a culture in your church that helps multiply your ministry as you give your ministry away is hard work. It requires, as Paul points out, that we warn and that we teach, and that we do all this through labor and striving. But we do all of this, as the text reminds us, because someday we are going to stand before Jesus, and we are going to be surrounded with those whom we had the privilege of leading. And as hard as our work is, as challenging as the biblical responsibility may be, I cannot help but be moved, nearly to tears, as I consider the biblical picture, the moment, that we present to Jesus those who have been under our responsibility, and we present them as having grown in Him and we watch as He completes the work, making them completely mature. As the old hymn says, "Oh what a day that will be." This heavenly vision was fuel for Paul's ministry. We need this kind of fuel because there are days, really difficult days, when our desire will run low and our confidence will be undercut. On those days, we have to look to that heavenly vision and be reminded of our divine calling and the blessing that it is.

May God use you to level your church. And as you give your ministry away, may God be glorified through your efforts.

Even as you stumble along, may God give you fruit and may you be encouraged as you bring Him glory. May we say, along with Paul, in his letter to the church at Rome:

> For from him and through him
> and to him are all things.
> To him be the glory forever. Amen. (Rom. 11:36)

ACKNOWLEDGMENTS

This book is a testimony to God's patience in my (Micah's) life as I have stumbled along in church leadership. God has taught me to love His church and to love serving her, in spite of my leadership failures. I owe everything to Him. Beyond God, no one has modeled unconditional love to me as much as my wife, Tracy, has. She is the closest person I know to being like Jesus. I love you Tracy, and I love (and am amazed) that you love me. I owe a big thanks to my kids, Sarah Grace, Kessed Noel, and Haddon for being patient with me as Dad devoted time to put these thoughts down on paper. Thank you to my dad and mom, who have taught me to trust God and walk by faith. Thank you to the people who make up Brainerd Baptist Church. I love you, and I love serving you. Thank you to Jeremy for helping me think through the ideas in this book. Your sharp thinking and incredible writing are gifts to me and the church. Thank you to Daniel Im, who pushed me years ago to take this idea and flesh it out more. If it were not for his encouragement, this book would have not happened. Finally, thank you to the incredible team at Moody. Drew and Kevin have been a dream team to work with.

I (Jeremy) would like to thank God for turning my prodigal story into one of love for the church. I want to thank my dad for his quiet faithfulness to lead by example—not only in our family but also in the two churches he served for nearly forty years. Well done, good and faithful servant. Thanks to my local church pastors over the years who personally invested in me and influenced my view of ministry—Bryant, Mike, David, Ken, Jon, Daryl, and Micah. Thanks to two friends who help me think outside the box and dream of what the church can be—Adam and Daniel. Thank you to the amazing team at Moody—Drew and Kevin in particular for trusting and guiding us in the process of writing this book. We pray that any good on these pages will bless countless pastors and churches for generations to come and anything else will be quickly forgotten! Finally, thank you to my wife, Amanda, for being the constant reminder of God's grace as the companion by my side no matter where the Lord places us. I pray that we would never separate "ministry" from our daily lives and that our girls—Adalyn, Ella, and Katy Jane—would grow up to love the church family and live on mission.

NOTES

Chapter 1: Rethinking Leadership

1. Some of the material from pages 14–24 is adapted from Micah Fries, "Equip, Don't Enable," Reaching Africa's Unreached, April 18, 2013, https://reaching africasunreached.org/2013/04/18/2637/.
2. Jim Putman, *Church Is a Team Sport: A Championship Strategy for Doing Ministry Together* (Grand Rapids: Baker Books, 2008).
3. Colin Marshall and Tony Payne, *The Trellis and the Vine: The Ministry Mind-Shift That Changes Everything* (Kingsford, Australia: Matthias Media, 2009).

Chapter 2: Reframing Leadership Success

1. Timothy Keller, *Center Church: Doing Balanced, Gospel-Centered Ministry in Your City* (Grand Rapids: Zondervan, 2012), 13–14.
2. For an in-depth look at D-Group ministry, see Robby Gallaty, *Rediscovering Discipleship: Making Jesus' Final Words Our First Work* (Grand Rapids: Zondervan, 2015).
3. See Chris McChesney, Sean Covey, and Jim Huling, *The 4 Disciplines of Execution: Achieving Your Wildly Important Goals* (New York: Free Press, 2012) 23–43.

Chapter 3: The Danger of Professionalism

1. Ed Stetzer, "Laypeople and the Mission of God, Part 1 -- Killing the Clergy-Laity Caste System," *The Exchange*, July 17, 2012, https://www .christianitytoday.com/edstetzer/2012/july/laypeople-and-mission-of-god-part-1--killing-clergy.html.

Chapter 4: The Danger of Materialism

1. Dietrich Bonhoeffer, *The Cost of Discipleship* (London: SCM Press, 1948/2001), 44.

Chapter 5: The Danger of Independence

1. Patrick Gillespie, "Intuit: Gig Economy Is 34% of US Workforce," CNN Business, March 24, 2017, https://money.cnn.com/2017/05/24/news/ economy/gig-economy-intuit/index.html.
2. Brian Fikkert and Kelly M. Kapic, *Becoming Whole: Why the Opposite of Poverty Isn't the American Dream* (Chicago: Moody, 2019), chapter 4.
3. J. Hampton Keathley III, "The Trinity (Triunity) of God," Bible.org, May 18, 2004, https://bible.org/article/trinity-triunity-god.

Chapter 6: The Danger of the Super Pastor

1. Henri Nouwen, *The Living Reminder: Service and Prayer in the Ministry of Jesus Christ* (New York: HarperCollins, 1977).

2. For more on this, see Stephen L. Woodworth, "The Ministry of Absence," *CT Pastors,* September 2018, https://www.christianitytoday.com/pastors/2018/september-web-exclusives/ministry-of-absence-henri-nouwen .html.

3. Some of the material from pages 101–107 is adapted from Micah Fries, "God Didn't Call You to Be a Super-Pastor," MicahFries.com, September 30, 2015, https://micahfries.com/micah-fries/god-didnt-call-you-to-be-a-super-pastor.

4. Justin Taylor, "Tim Keller | Our Identity: The Christian Alternative to Late Modernity's Story," The Gospel Coalition, November 12, 2015, https://www .thegospelcoalition.org/blogs/justin-taylor/tim-keller-our-identity-the-christian-alternative-to-late-modernitys-story/.

Chapter 8: Lead Like Moses: Never Do What You Can Delegate

1. Dhati Lewis, *Among Wolves: Disciple-Making in the City* (Nashville: B&H, 2017), 75.

2. Quoted in Jonathan C. Liu, "Developing a Pastoral Leadership Guide In Light of the Biblical Teachings and the Contemporary Management Concepts" (DMin Thesis, Liberty Baptist Theological Seminary, 1995), https:// digitalcommons.liberty.edu/cgi/viewcontent.cgi?article=1260&context= doctoral.

3. Markham Heid, "You Asked: How Many Friends Do I Need?" *Time,* March 18, 2015, http://time.com/3748090/friends-social-health/?iid=time_speed.

Chapter 9: Lead Like Paul: Model and Mentor

1. Alvin L. Reid and George G. Robinson, *With: A Practical Guide to Informal Mentoring and Intentional Disciple Making* (Spring Hill, TN: Rainer Publishing, 2016).

Chapter 10: Lead Like Timothy: Train and Deploy

1. Bob Smietana, "LifeWay Research: Americans Are Fond of the Bible, Don't Actually Read It," LifeWay Research, April 25, 2017, https://lifewayresearch .com/2017/04/25/lifeway-research-americans-are-fond-of-the-bible-dont-actually-read-it/.

2. In his book *No Silver Bullets: Five Small Shifts That Will Transform Your Ministry* (Nashville: B&H, 2017), Daniel Im summarizes research and practical wisdom from consulting with church leaders throughout North America and in contexts around the world, identifying four general styles of church ministry philosophies—copy cat, hippie, silver bullet, intentional. We'd propose the same general categories exist for leadership development and education/ discipleship.

3. James A. Smith Sr., "Theological Education Happens in the Local Church," *Southern Seminary Magazine,* Spring 2016, http://equip.sbts.edu/publications/ magazine/theological-education-happens-in-the-local-church-2/.

4. "2018 State of American Theology Study: Research Report," LifeWay Research, http://lifewayresearch.com/wp-content/uploads/2018/10/Ligonier-State-of-Theology-2018-White-Paper.pdf.

WHAT TO DO WHEN THEY SAY THEY'RE CHRISTIAN BUT DON'T KNOW JESUS

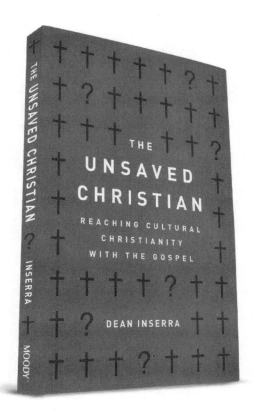

MOODY Publishers®

From the Word to Life®

The Unsaved Christian equips you to confront cultural Christianity with honesty, compassion, and grace, whether you're doing it from the pulpit or the pews. If you've ever felt stuck or unsure how to minister to someone who identifies as Christian but still needs Jesus, this book is for you.

978-0-8024-1880-7 | also available as an eBook

AS A PASTOR, DO YOU FEEL LIKE YOU'RE WEARING TOO MANY HATS?

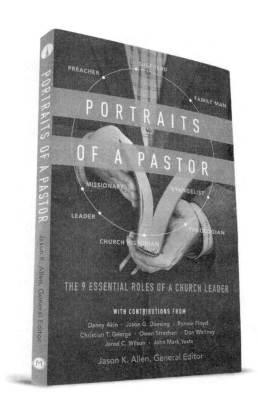

DISCOVER WHY THE FUNDAMENTALS OF THE REFORMATION STILL MATTER TODAY

Sola is a winsome, inspiring introduction to the five pillars of the Reformation, showing not just what they are but why they're important for the Christian life today. Edited and compiled by Jason Allen, *Sola* will illuminate these core truths and it may just get you excited about nerdy Latin phrases.

978-0-8024-1873-9 | also available as an eBook